"We didn't decide to w... how the world how devastating agoraphobia can be or to air our grievances at the years of pain we endured while unable to find reasonable help. Instead, we have chosen to write it for the agoraphobia victim, or potential victim, who wants honest answers and a tried-and-true plan for overcoming this overwhelming problem. We did, and you most certainly can."

—Ann Seagrave and Faison Covington

FREE FROM FEARS IS . . .

"Excellent . . . of great value for people suffering from anxiety, panic disorders, and agoraphobia. It conveys in a personal and readable way valuable insights and practical techniques that will help people to recognize and accept their symptoms . . . [It] captures much of the spirit, warmth, and value of the CHAANGE program."

—Ari Kiev, M.D.,
Director, Life Strategy Workshops

ANN SEAGRAVE and FAISON COVINGTON are the founders and directors of CHAANGE, the Center for Help for Agoraphobia/Anxiety through New Growth Experiences, which has been recognized by the Phobia Society of America. Their pioneering work has been covered by major publications and national television networks across the country. They live in Charlotte, North Carolina.

POCKET BOOKS, a division of Simon & Schuster Inc.
1230 Avenue of the Americas, New York, NY 10020

Copyright © 1987 by Ann Seagrave and Faison Covington

Library of Congress Catalog Card Number: 87-2553

ISBN: 0-671-66642-8

First Pocket Books paperback printing January 1989

10 9 8 7 6 5 4 3 2 1

POCKET and colophon are trademarks of
Simon & Schuster Inc.

Cover design by Mike Stromberg

Printed in the U.S.A.

FREE FROM FEARS

NEW HELP FOR ANXIETY, PANIC AND AGORAPHOBIA

Ann Seagrave and
Faison Covington

POCKET BOOKS

New York   London   Toronto   Sydney   Tokyo

▼▼▼▼▼▼▼

Acknowledgments

▲▲▲▲▲▲▲

The authors would like to express their thanks, gratitude and affection to the following people who enabled them to complete this book: to our husbands, Millard and Earl; Susie Abrams and Ann Hinson, who helped enormously with editing and typed till their fingers were numb; Laura Carpenter and Ann McNeil, who produced an atmosphere of unfailing encouragement and support; David Sparling, who never doubted we could do it; Diana and Sam Walden, great shipmates and dear companions; Sydny Weinberg Miner, our editor, who was unbelievably patient and reassuring; Betsy Nolan, our friend and literary agent; Dr. Lawrence Calhoun, Dr. Jim Selby, Susan Shaw, M.A., S.S.P., and Dr. Robin King, who helped us so much with technical matters and whose support was (and is) unending; the family and staff on the Chalet Club, Lake Lure, N.C., who, as a group, helped us as we wrote our book in their lovely surroundings—all of them were wonderful; to the thousands of individuals who suffered with agoraphobia and with whom we have had contact over the past years; and finally, to our families—we could not—and would not—have been able to do it without you! Thanks.

Contents

FREE FROM FEARS

Chapter

1

▼▼▼▼▼▼▼

We Can Help You

▲▲▲▲▲▲▲▲

NOBODY KNOWS BETTER about agoraphobia and the body-shaking panic it produces than an agoraphobic. Physicians, psychiatrists, psychologists, social workers and ministers can understand the condition in the abstract, and offer the best of their years of training to help you work through your miseries, but they can't *know* and *feel* what you are suffering unless it has happened to them. We are writing this book about agoraphobia from firsthand knowledge. We both suffered long and hard with the condition, recovered completely and have spent the last eight years helping other victims conquer their anxieties. We believe that we can motivate you to try something different, to enter a once-frightening situation and to change habitual patterns of behavior, because we have total empathy as well as a proved system of recovery. We didn't decide to write this book to show the world how devastating agoraphobia can be or to air our grievances at the years of pain we endured while unable to find reasonable help. Instead, we have chosen to write it for the agoraphobia victim, or potential victim, who wants honest answers and a tried-and-true plan for overcoming this overwhelming problem.

A six-year, $15 million study conducted by the National Institute of Mental Health (NIMH) reports anxiety disorders—phobias, panic disorders and obsessive-compulsive disorders—to be the most widespread of mental difficulties in the United States: 8.3 percent of the adult population are thought to suffer in this way. Only a little over one-fifth had recently sought professional help, and then more often from their medical doctor than from a mental-health professional. Before this study, the accepted wisdom was that depression was the number one mental-health problem; now it is known that panic and acute anxiety are more prevalent.

Some people have a hard time pinpointing exactly how and when their lives changed direction, but this is not true for anyone who has ever experienced panic. Ann can remember the exact date, the hour, the weather conditions, the clothes she had on her back and precisely how she felt the very first time she suffered an anxiety attack. Faison remembers her first episode in just the same vivid detail, and can recount it as though it had happened yesterday, although in truth, many years have come and gone.

When we first met, we were both nervous because neither of us had ever met a fellow agoraphobic and we didn't know what to expect. We were introduced by the counselor who had been helping us individually with our problem. Both of us had made good progress in therapy, and each of us had asked the therapist whether she was seeing anyone else with the same symptoms, hoping that we could learn more about ourselves. It was a tremendous relief to know that somebody else in the world had felt the terror, the depression and the loneliness—somebody who looked and acted perfectly normal in every way. Our luncheon meeting lasted until midnight as we compared everything about ourselves: who we were, who our parents were; our grandparents, our husbands, our likes and dislikes, our beliefs. It became apparent that there were just too many similarities for them not to have had some bearing on our developing the agoraphobic condition; our therapist also believed that they were significant.

Several weeks went by before we met again, but it was obvious from the way our second encounter began that we had both been giving thought to what we had learned. Did other agoraphobics fit our personality profile—and if so, how could they use that information?

As we worked at defining our personality patterns, we also spent time talking about the unsuccessful attempts we had made at recovery, and specifically why those efforts had proved unhelpful. We carefully examined the methods that had worked for us and discovered that there had been a clearly discernible system of progress for each of us. With help, we believed that on the basis of our years of experience both in and out of the condition, we could structure a process of value to others.

Once again we contacted our therapist and asked her to join us in designing a program for the successful treatment of agoraphobia. Before any of us could stop and think, we were hard at work. In July of 1979, *The Char-*

lotte Observer ran a lengthy and fairly dramatic account of our bouts with agoraphobia and what we hoped to offer our own community. None of us will ever forget the impact of our willingness to reveal the fears that had plagued us for years. The article ran in the Sunday-morning edition, and before the day was out, we had received two hundred fifty calls for help. Each caller was amazed that we had actually felt as he or she was feeling, and each person was vastly relieved to learn that there was a *name* for that condition and also a way out of it!

We spent the next few weeks on the phone, offering much empathy and reassurance and, often, just lending an understanding ear. The sheer numbers of callers in our own city indicated to us that there must be thousands and thousands of sufferers across the nation who were desperately seeking help. With each person who signed up for our group process, we prayed that we were right in our new and unique approach. By the time our first group of ten had reached the midpoint in their sessions, we realized that our program was proving to be even more successful than we had dreamed. We became exhilarated by the obvious desire among agoraphobics to actively *do* something about their condition rather than continue to allow it to govern their lives. This willingness to learn, to understand and finally to conquer agoraphobia is nothing less than inspirational.

The name of our organization is CHAANGE—an acronym for *C*enter for *H*elp for *A*goraphobia/*A*nxiety through *N*ew *G*rowth *E*xperiences. Since that first group of ten agoraphobics who began our program in July of 1979, more than six thousand individuals have participated in our treatment program. Early in 1980, we developed our fifteen-session process into tape cassettes, utilizing therapeutic dialogue between a therapist and a recovered agoraphobic, rather than recording sets of instructions. Each weekly session is accompanied by specific homework assignments, and the sessions are interconnected, with one week building toward the next. This step-by-step approach guarantees that goals will be reached and that complete recovery can be expected. Program participants receive their sessions either at home, for work on their own, or from a CHAANGE-affiliated therapist who has been trained to use our methods. Careful monitoring by the clinical staff in Charlotte ensures that the "in home" participant receives the same quality help as does the individual who receives his program session at weekly meetings with an associated therapist.

Before CHAANGE, and before our own recoveries from agoraphobia, we both searched out and read every book on the subject we could find. Our thinking was that if we could read enough or understand enough, then surely we could work toward a solution of the problem. The books we read were often confusing, sometimes hopeful, but never definitive. What we were looking for in a book was help—the kind of help that we could put into practice; but usually we were presented instead with more and more information about the condition itself. Most articles and books about agoraphobia by physicians and therapists seemed only to be written to impress other professionals, rather than to offer concrete suggestions for recovery. We became dedicated to the idea of writing a book that could be used as a process of help in much the same way that our program was created. We ask all CHAANGE participants to commit themselves to doing the work set forth for them in their fifteen-week process. We are going to ask you to do the same as you work through this book.

In writing it, we have drawn on our own experiences in outlining and detailing skills for you to learn and tools for you to use. Trusting that the two of us are giving you good advice, that we've been there ourselves, that we have tried and succeeded, that we have stumbled occasionally but have nevertheless moved forward will set an optimistic tone for the work ahead. We are not going to talk *at* you, but we are going to talk *to* you in exactly the same way we wish we had been talked to many years ago. We will never tell you that the job of recovery was easy for us, or that it will be for you. But we can promise you that your hard work will pay off well beyond the conquering of fearful feelings.

We are delighted to be working with you and excited about all the steps that we will be taking together. By the time you have finished this book, you will know almost as much about us as we know about ourselves. We established that same rapport with our program participants years ago, and we believe that being totally open and honest about who we are, how we think, how we act and react will help you open doors for yourself. Pointing out our misconceptions and the mistakes we made along the way will lighten your load. Giving you clear examples of what worked best for us will give you a direction to follow. We are not, nor will we ever be, perfect in any of our approaches to day-to-day living; but we have found the key that unlocks agoraphobia, and we are passing it along to you.

Chapter

2

▾▾▾▾▾▾▾

What Is Agoraphobia?

▲▲▲▲▲▲▲▲

THE RANDOM HOUSE DICTIONARY gives a very simplistic and quick definition of agoraphobia: "an abnormal fear of being in an open space." The DSM-III—the *Diagnostic & Statistical Manual* put out by the American Psychiatric Association—says that this condition is "the marked fear of being alone or being in public places from which escape might be difficult or help not available in case of incapacitation." Neither of these definitions describes what we are feeling in a way that is particularly comforting or helpful. Ann realized that she had agoraphobia when she read a magazine article by a woman who seemed, as she wrote of her fears, to be talking about Ann herself. We have since found that most of us are diagnosed in the same way—by chance.

Almost without exception, agoraphobia begins with an unexpected and unexplained panic attack. More specifically, this first attack should be labeled a "terror reaction," because our bodies act in a way that is, for us, terrifying. Ann's first episode of panic occurred as she was driving down a familiar stretch of road. As she describes the attack: "Suddenly, and for no apparent reason, my body went berserk. At first I thought I was going to throw up, but before I could even think what to do about that, a host of other horrifying sensations began to surface. I became hot and sweaty, although I was shaking as if cold. My vision blurred and my feet went so numb that I honestly didn't believe I could brake to stop the car. I felt totally out of control of myself and my body; I ended up becoming hysterical."

There seems to be no end to the ways in which our bodies can react during a panic attack. No sooner do we rid ourselves of one nasty symptom than another crops up. We stay on the alert for fear that the very next reaction will be the one that causes us to make fools of ourselves, go totally crazy or drop dead. There is little wonder that we are afraid of these attacks, since just *some* of the physical symptoms may be: dry mouth; dizziness; nausea; an urgent need to relieve both bladder and bowels; numbness in feet, legs, hands and arms; uncontrollable shaking; a sense of unreality; blurred or tunnel vision; heart palpitations; tightness of chest; hyperventilation; neck spasms; inability to think clearly; loss of balance; sense of dread. There may be as many varieties of anxiety reactions as there are people who have them. Who in the world would choose to put himself through *one* of these feelings, let alone several such chillers at once?

The answer? Lots of people. Parachutists, race-car drivers, roller-coaster fanatics and even joggers are seeking an adrenaline rush. Adrenaline flows when we are exercising, when we get excited, when we lose our tempers and, of course, when we are afraid. To pump adrenaline is our body's natural reaction to danger; the effect speaks loudly and clearly, letting us know that we are alive and ready for whatever is coming. Without a healthy shot of adrenaline, our reaction time would be considerably slower. The moment that we think, "All is well!" the flow of adrenaline subsides and our body's reactions cease. We become afraid of this normal, natural reaction only when there doesn't seem to be any sensible *reason* for it.

Those of us who take an easy view of anxiety feelings as our body's natural reaction to stress don't develop agoraphobia. The rest of us simply didn't recognize the overload of stress when it came along. Stress is a part of all our lives. There are "good" stresses (the birth of a baby, a promotion, a move to a new house) and "bad" stresses (the loss of a job, illness, death of a loved one), and each of us handles her share of these stresses pretty well. It is when we fill our "stress cup" to overflowing that our body's protective system steps in and gives us a message. That first panic attack is merely our body's way of telling us to take a look at ourselves and our environment and to evaluate our needs under the strained circumstances. For many of us, there were lesser body warnings all along that we ignored or misinterpreted, such as insomnia, eyestrain, crying, muscle tension or generalized moderate anxiety. Sometimes all we need is a little rest or recreation to keep us from overloading. This is what we hope you will recognize when you read this book.

Ann's second panic attack took place almost exactly like the first one. She recalls: "Two weeks later, I was in the car, running a mundane errand, oblivious to the fact that the stresses present earlier were still very much with me. Again I felt as though I were about to die or have a heart attack, and again I felt compelled to stop my car and call my husband to come from work and rescue me."

It was after this experience that she learned a new kind of behavior: avoidance. This term is widely used in the psychological field to describe what happens when fearful feelings begin to restrict one's ability to move about freely. It never occurred to Ann that she was establishing an avoidance behavior. She was much too interested in forestalling those awful feelings she believed might lead to a heart attack or stroke, or that might cause her to totally lose control in some way. It seemed logical to her to curtail any activity that would cause her so much panic.

Earl and Ann were married on Valentine's Day in 1975. Earl, then fifty-five, had custody of two of his five children from a previous marriage, and Ann, age thirty-one, came equipped with a five-year-old son. Everything went smoothly for six months; then it became necessary to pack up their household and move.

Ann states: "Rockford, Illinois, is where my agoraphobia began, and though I recognize that the town had absolutely nothing to do with my fears, I have never been able to think of Rockford without cringing. To say that Earl and I were under stress would be the understatement of the century, so I want to outline for you some of the events which preceded that first devastating blow to my stability.

"Our neighborhood was a small, two-block affair that appeared to have been dropped into the middle of the Illinois cornfields. There was farmland all around us, and everything seemed flat and uninviting. As soon as we moved into our house, the weather turned cold and the neighbors moved indoors, where they stayed for the next six months. In an attempt to meet people, I volunteered for everything. I became a library helper at grammar school, a reading assistant at high school, a volunteer at St. Anthony's Hospital. I felt awkward and ill at ease every time I arrived to do my jobs. Half of the time no one could understand a word I said because of my Southern accent, and the other half of the time I couldn't understand my co-workers or helpers because of their abrupt Midwestern manner. The more uncomfortable I felt, the harder it was for me to make friends, and soon I found myself blaming others, concluding that Midwesterners lacked warmth and understanding. I was just too frustrated to give them or myself a fair chance.

"It soon became apparent that Earl was not at all happy about this move either; he wasn't getting along with the people who had acquired his business and his services. He felt he had to stick it out, though, knowing that our financial security lay with the success of this venture. Money was tight for us and getting more precious by the second. I was scared, and I think that Earl was scared too.

"There was never a moment of peace, of quietly reading a book, privately taking a bath or just taking a long walk on a snowy day. I was afraid that if I let down for one minute, I would never get myself going again. I was scared and homesick and overwhelmed, and I didn't feel I had the right to feel that way. Shouldn't I, of all people, be able to handle all this? If I couldn't, then something was mighty wrong."

Once we have survived several panic attacks, instinct tells us to seek out places where these episodes don't occur. Before we realize it, we are avoiding more and more of those situations which might cause us trouble. "What if I have an attack in the store?" "What if I can't find the exit door at the movies?" "What if they call on me to speak at the meeting?" These are all frightening thoughts, and to keep them from becoming a reality, we make excuses and politely say "No, thank you." The more we do this, the more severe the problem becomes. It is a short step from not wanting to drive to avoiding all out-of-the-home activities.

It is in this way that the home can become a refuge. Much has been written about agoraphobia as the "housebound condition," and much has been made of the fact that occasionally people—both men and women—can and do become housebound. Many people suffering acute anxiety develop "safe" places, or places where in the past they've felt less anxious and more reassured, more able to get help if necessary or just less likely to become publicly embarrassed. Usually that safe place is our own home.

The process of becoming "housebound," or developing any places where safety is felt, is one that slowly evolves over the first few weeks or months of the severe anxiety condition. The suffering person adopts this pattern of behavior as a last alternative for dealing constructively with the anxiety. We just don't know what else to do, and often doctors, friends, relatives and ministers have been equally stumped. If the outside world continually seems to precipitate the frantic and painful feelings of anxiety and even panic, we eventually avoid that pain altogether until we learn ways to approach it more productively.

Most agoraphobics, in addition to establishing "safe" places, also imbue certain people with protector status. These people are often referred to as "safe" people or "support" people. It is not at all unusual for someone to call CHAANGE prior to coming to group and ask, "Is it all right for me to bring my sister along? She is my support person." Or, "I can't come to group unless my wife is with me. She is my safe person." These phrases are ones used by agoraphobics in CHAANGE groups all over the country. A person in Houston and a person in Chicago, hearing about groups for the first time, will call and use identical words in describing their need to have someone with them if they have developed the habit of a "safe" person.

Like the "safe place," a "safe person" is an attempt to manage anxiety by having someone around who can be counted on in an emergency. This person can rush you off to the emergency room; this person will sit with you and tell you that you are not crazy. This person becomes someone who, when it becomes necessary, will silently usher you out of a movie theater, or will leave a restaurant without finishing a meal.

Sometimes a "support person" is an understanding, patient, nonjudgmental family member or friend who is ever-willing to bear the hardships of being with an agoraphobic. But just as frequently, the "support person" is someone who is judgmental, who does not fully understand what is going on, who causes more anxiety by castigating the agoraphobic after hearing a doctor say for the twelfth time, "There is nothing wrong with you."

A safe place or safe person is never a real answer to the problem, but rather an attempt at temporary relief. No one we have ever met would be content to live "housebound" for the rest of his life. Likewise, no one we have ever talked with or heard from by letter feels O.K. about being accompanied through life by a well-meaning parent or spouse (or child in some cases, or dog). It simply isn't a full existence. Those of us who have lived that way for a month or decade are ever looking for that thing which will allow us to break the constraints that bind us. It never occurs to us that our own behavior might be keeping us bound so, and that we have *learned* this behavior.

If a baby is spanked every time he ventures close to an electrical outlet, he soon learns to stay away. The shock that our bodies repeatedly gave us, for which we could find no physical explanation, taught us a lesson in avoidance in the same way we learned to avoid the outlet. Our avoidance behavior pattern is a learned habit which feels more comfortable than the alternative.

We become so sensitized to the early warning signals of anxiety that we tend to read almost every body signal as a cue to an impending attack. After some months of struggling with chronic anxiety, Ann remembers: "I got to the point that I could absolutely not tell the difference between a physical malady and the symptoms of anxiety. Even if my temperature read 102 degrees, I was not certain whether the dizziness and sweating were coming from that or from the panic attacks I had been experiencing for months. My habit became one of overreacting and of fearing every single body message and body sensation. I was no longer sure of my instincts, and I had learned to mistrust my body.'' We can become frightened to such a degree that we learn to monitor every twitch, every ache, and it is in that way that we often scare ourselves needlessly.

Now let's look at what has really taken place in the early stages of agoraphobia; the answer is not nearly so complicated as it may at first appear. Ann had a physical reaction—better known as a panic attack—to an overload of some very real stresses in her life. Your first panic attack was no different, and you, like Ann, became extremely frightened by your body's responses. If you had experienced only one such episode, you probably could have put it out of your mind. The fact that such episodes were repeated taught you to avoid any situation which might bring on those terrifying physical symptoms.

We can now define agoraphobia with more understanding. The word describes severe anxiety, as well as a phobia which is complex.* The condition is a *learned* one in which the sufferer has developed avoidance patterns because of the fear of losing control, going crazy, becoming embarrassed, having a heart attack or dying. Because this condition is learned, it can be unlearned. We can teach ourselves to be unafraid much more easily and successfully than we taught ourselves to fear.

---

* In a simple phobia, such as a fear of snakes, there is one cue; in a complex phobia, there are many places and things that can trigger the anxiety response.

Chapter

3

▼▼▼▼▼▼▼

Why Did This Happen to Me?

▲▲▲▲▲▲▲▲▲

LET US PUT your mind at rest from the very beginning. The personality that has the propensity for severe anxiety is a fine, creative and likable one; above all, it is a personality with enormous strengths. We have worked and spoken with thousands of people who have suffered with this condition, and neither of us has ever met or talked with an agoraphobic whom we didn't immediately like. We know that you have probably been concerned and worried that something "wrong" with you caused this problem. Understanding the development of your condition and why it happened to you is a helpful start in the process of letting go of the fear of agoraphobia.

Psychoanalysts like to think that the "why" is most important in dealing with this condition, and behaviorists argue that looking too hard for reasons only slows recovery. We believe that there is a healthy spot somewhere between these two approaches. We're going to spend time dealing with the issue of "Why did this happen to me?" before we even discuss making some important behavior changes. We suspect that you are very much like us, and that you won't rest until you can figure out for yourself just exactly what has gone on in your life that produced the anxious you.

No one we know simply accepted agoraphobia as his or her fate. What a relief it is to find out that there is an explanation that is not fraught with words like "maladaptive," "emotionally unstable" or "hopelessly neurotic." There really is a reason that we—and you—developed agoraphobia. It has everything to do with who we are.

INHERITED CHARACTERISTICS

People who develop agoraphobia are born with creative intelligence and an abundance of sensitivity to all kinds of stimuli. You were not the baby who peacefully slept through a party going on in the next room. Even as a small child, you reacted strongly to loud noises, to bright lights, to heat and cold and often to medication. This hyperawareness or keen sensitivity can also be interpreted as the biological predisposition to agoraphobia. It is important for you to recognize and accept your inherent intelligence and sensitivity. However, it is equally helpful to realize that your environment during your early years also played a role in setting you up for later difficulties with acute anxiety.

ALCOHOLISM/INSTABILITY

Often, agoraphobics have grown up without the benefit of positive role models. The most obvious example is that of growing up with an alcoholic family member; we have seen a high statistical correlation between alcoholism in the family and agoraphobia.* However, there are other situations which can cause this emotional upheaval and deprive a child of a reliable support system.

If you don't have an alcoholic parent, the odds are that you experienced other kinds of instability. Financial insecurity, abusiveness, neglect, the early death of a parent or any such situation could have left you feeling scared, insecure and out of control. In order to survive in a world that often seems to be toppling down, the child of an alcoholic may develop a "take charge" attitude. Ann says that in order to manage her insecurity, she became a bossy and aggressive little girl, constantly trying to prove that she was smarter and braver than anyone else. Creating and maintaining this image of control was the most important motivating factor in her daily existence; everything she did, on the playground, at home or at school, reflected her need to be in control. She had to provide her own sense of stability and kept up this pretense for many years. She thought it served her pretty well. Faison took the opposite approach in her efforts to establish control of her environment. Rather than assertively "taking charge," she hid her feelings from

---

* An early study (1979) of thirty-one CHAANGE graduates suggested that 70 percent of agoraphobics were reared by, or around, alcoholic family members. Clinical observation through the years has strengthened this supposition.

the world and shielded herself from decision-making. She was an introspective child who spent much of her time worrying.

Many agoraphobics were sexually or physically abused as children and as young adults. For them, this was the early pattern that led to feelings of insecurity, guilt and an altered sense of self-worth, their feelings of being "different" and of having something to hide.

SEPARATION ANXIETY

Separation anxiety is the other primary factor in the psychological development of agoraphobia. Little children are frightened and upset when they realize that Mama or Daddy is nowhere in sight. Your comfort level as a toddler was in direct relationship to the availability of your parents. We don't have a mature sense of time as little folks, so hearing "I'll be right back" can feel the same as hearing "This is goodbye forever and ever." Childhood fears of this kind are known as separation anxiety and are experienced by every child. The trouble is that those of us who later become victims of the anxiety reaction happened to have a double dose of separation anxiety as small children, which helped make us more susceptible to our later uneasy feelings.

Ann remembered making the weekly trip to the dry cleaner's with her mother: "If she left me in the car, I would have a fit even though I could see her through the big glass window at the front of the store. On the days I was allowed to go inside with her, I would stand behind her and bury my head in the fabric of her skirt. I can't imagine why I was so afraid at the dry cleaner's, but I do know that I had a fear that my mama would disappear behind the huge load of shirts and suits she was carrying, and would never be seen again.

"I had a severe panic attack when I was about six years old, though it was years and years later before I realized what had happened to me. My grammar school was about four neighborhood blocks from our house, and one day I stayed after school to work with my teacher. I told her that my mother had given me permission to walk home by myself. She had, of course, *not* given me permission, and I had never walked that far alone in my life. Well, off I started on my adventure, and crossing the first street I had done pretty well, when the street suddenly grew in my imagination, and I just knew that I would never see home again. I began to walk very fast, with little legs shaking and heart pounding. I thought about stopping at the house of a neighbor, but I didn't want anyone to know how much trouble I had gotten myself into. I began to run, and the faster I ran, the more frightened I became. Soon I was crying at the top of my lungs, and somebody heard me and came flying out to see what all the commotion was about. A very nice lady gathered me up, gave me cookies and juice, and called my mother. I will never forget how glad I was to see Mom's old green Plymouth pull up; but my relief was no compensation for the embarrassment I felt for not having been able to walk home from school all by myself."

Some children's separation anxiety can stem from over-protectiveness on the part of a worrying parent. A parent who is overprotective of a child tends to be a parent who is a worrier him- or herself, and who opts for the easy way out: it is easier to forbid a child to venture out into the world than it is to spend the energy dealing with *parental* fears and worries. The child of an overprotective parent receives the message that he is not equipped to handle the world outside the home without the parent along. At the same time, this child has a role model who doesn't handle anxiety well. It is little wonder, then, that the overprotected child has difficulty leaving home and risking a life on his own in an adult world.

CRITICAL REARING

Adults who are severely anxious commonly felt judged and criticized as children. When parents (or older siblings, teachers or grandparents) seemed to praise us only when we performed well, we tended to become very critical of our own performance. Phrases like "If I make good grades, Mom and Dad will love me more," "If I hadn't complained, Mom wouldn't be sick," "If only I were prettier, I would be more popular" are common to those of us who have experienced severe anxiety and the background that often leads to it.

Children who are reared with harsh or constant criticism, spoken or unspoken, come to feel that there are perfect people in the world and that if they could somehow work a little harder, they too could be perfect (and loved). Ann says: "Often I would imitate someone whom I viewed as perfect, only to become unhappy when I fell short of my expectations."

EMOTIONAL REPRESSION

Many anxious people tend to repress their emotions, and for some of us this repression started early. In many of our homes, it was considered unthinkable to cry for no reason at all, or to feel rotten without there being a definable physical cause. Our feelings, so it seemed, were not valid, and they were never to be paraded for others to see. There wasn't much discussion in the family environment regarding emotional and physical needs. We didn't talk about sex, anger, depression or elation. Discussion of such subjects would have been considered "in poor taste." Consequently, we were very naïve about our feelings and about the workings of our minds and bodies. There were often times when we may have felt "crazy as a loon" and quite confused by our unruly feelings and thoughts.

When we mention this early-childhood naïveté, people often assume we're referring to a taboo on the discussion of sexual matters. However, the taboo on talking openly and candidly about your body and your feelings goes far beyond the simply sexual. In fact, it is this one trait which may have had more to do with your developing agoraphobia than anything else. Had you known about normal body reactions, you would not have ultimately been so frightened by your body's reaction to stress.

In addition to sexual expression, we find that the feelings most often repressed include: anger (especially at parents, other authority figures and venerable social institutions such as church and school); sadness and grief; curiosity and wonderment; disappointment; dislike and displeasure; fear; worry; depression or despondency. Because these feelings were not explored during childhood, and weren't felt and dealt with in a protected environment, many of us learned to fear such emotions or became guilty and worried about feeling them. We may sense that we are weak or sick in some way if we can't control each emotion and keep it modulated every minute of the day. To state the matter very simply, we are naïve about emotionality, and therefore don't quite know how to handle the normal ebb and flow of our feelings. It is a skill that we didn't learn, and one that had much to do with our fearful reaction to stress and anxiety later in our lives.

FEAR OF MENTAL ILLNESS

Many of us have stories to tell of childhood encounters with people we thought were "crazy" and frightening. The fear of insanity haunted both of us as children and we each grew up believing that losing one's mind was a fate worse than death. The fear of going crazy, being institutionalized and ostracized from society seems more ominous for agoraphobics than for less inner-directed individuals.

Agoraphobics fear that they will be unable to control their anxious feelings, just as crazy people appear unable to control their actions. We make the irrational assumption that anxiety or panic is the first step toward insanity, and that somehow we will be helpless to stop the progression. This belief, held over from childhood, has no real basis in fact: agoraphobia (anxiety and panic disorder) does not now, nor has it ever, implied mental illness.

THE ADULT WE BECOME

A child reared in an unstable environment often grows into an adult who views control as the ultimate asset. Children with a large dose of separation anxiety can doubt their own abilities to perform credibly in young adulthood. Critical parenting breeds judgmental offspring. Repression begets thwarted emotions. Unrealistic fears produce *more* unrealistic fears. The sensitive child unconsciously develops mechanisms for coping as he makes his way toward responsible membership in adult society. One of the most frequently employed of these mechanisms is perfectionism.

PERFECTIONISM

Because following the rules seemed so important to us as children, as adults we imposed on ourselves a code of "shoulds" and "rules" that was overwhelming. Some of Ann's were: "I should go to church every Sunday." "I should look good and arrive on time for everything." "I should plan and prepare three delicious and well-balanced meals daily for my family." "I should do charity work in my community and good deeds for my fellow man." "I should be generous to a fault and never complain." "I should be successful in my business and on top of all situations." She remembers: "When we were living in Illinois, I fixed four bag lunches for school every morning. The kids would have been thrilled with a peanut butter sandwich and some chips; but oh, no, perfect moms send well-balanced and aesthetically beautiful lunches in carefully folded, crisp brown bags to school for their perfectly clean, well-mannered children to eat. Did I care if my kids liked or even ate those wonderful feasts? Heck, no. I was boiling the eggs, slicing the fruit and deviling the ham just in case another mother might happen to witness my child opening his bag and suddenly be filled with awe for the superb woman who so obviously knew the meaning of the word 'mother.' Appearance was everything to me. I did everything on the basis of how I wanted to look to others. I let the fundamentals of life slide right by, and all for the sake of appearing to be on top of the world."

All of us are like that to some extent. We may never leave room for human imperfection in our own lives, even though we can see that others don't take themselves quite so seriously. *We need to be in control of everything*—our jobs, our homes, our relationships, our environments. *Dependable?* You bet we are, and *competent*, too. How many times have you heard yourself say "I can handle it," and then gone and done just that? It may wear us to a frazzle, but handle it we do. Not only do we take on too much, but we also believe that we should be able to take it on calmly and serenely, suffering no stressful aftereffects. We truly believe that we "should" be able to direct the evacuation of an entire city with zero anticipation or anxiety; with hands dry and folded loosely behind our backs.

We often believe that we "can't cope" or that we "aren't able to cope" with life when we are in fact coping with almost everything. It may well be that we are not using a productive or positive system of coping, but we are taking care of the necessities and responding to what needs to be done nevertheless. It is important to know that the anxious individual is characterized by nothing more strongly than his or her need to cope with every situation. Even those who are limited in their ability to travel or shop can see that they really *are* dealing with the daily requirements of their lives, though just not in the easiest and most joyful manner. In fact, they are *over*-coping! They won't miss work or their turn in a car pool unless they are running a temperature of 103 degrees and the doctor has been called in. Goofing off for the sake of goofing off is simply not an option. They either don't relax at all, or do it with such feelings of guilt that they are left anxious and worried. It never occurs to them that they can be worn out without having a physical illness.

INTELLECTUALIZING/WORRYING

We rarely listen to what our bodies have to say to us because we put *all* importance on what our *heads* say. We follow the dictates of our thoughts to the extent that we ignore the needs of our bodies. In other words, we see absolutely no connection between our minds and our bodies, and try to deny that our bodies even *exist* in any important way. Our tendency toward intellectualizing spawns the worry habit.

Most—if not all—agoraphobics are worriers. Worrying is a habit, and like all other habits, it begins innocently enough. We *learn* to worry from people who feel compelled not only to worry, but often to *share* their worry with us. It is not at all uncommon for an accomplished worrier to believe that his worrying holds some sort of magical power. Ann believed in that kind of magic for a long time. She thought that her worrying might keep something awful from happening.

There may be a sense of compulsiveness about this incessant fretting; it is almost as though we *should* worry in order to forestall disaster. For example, you may feel that you are not acting as a concerned citizen unless you conscientiously worry about nuclear proliferation. It may never occur to you that it does no *good* to worry; you just feel that you *should*.

There is a world of difference between worry and concern. To be *concerned* about an issue, person or possibility means to devote to that subject a measure of attention or vigilance. It means that you are conscientious to the extent that you *do* whatever is possible. Worry means that you don't do; you *stew*. If everyone in the world stews about nuclear proliferation, nothing changes. If, on the other hand, everyone is concerned, caring and responsible, then we have a different world altogether. So often we confuse worry with caring when in fact worry may preclude caring, responsible behavior.

You may not feel compelled to worry over anything so global, focusing instead on your own health. The reason for this is that *all* agoraphobics are highly suggestible: easily stimulated, sensitive and imaginative. They are keenly empathic, sensing both the pleasure and the pain that others may display or describe. They are thus likely to add to their own cache of symptoms by taking on those of someone else. The agoraphobic condition intensifies the tendency toward suggestibility because the focus has become symptom-oriented. Incessant worry expends precious energy and can lead to exhaustion.

Additionally, intellectualizers/worriers tend to be overly concerned with others' opinions of them. They are likely to interpret any criticism as a judgment. Forgetting past injustices and insults is difficult because they want so much to be right, to please, to be "better than." As a result, they may develop an enormous *fear of rejection*. "I can't let anyone know that I can make mistakes, lose my temper or wring my hands, because as soon as they realize that I have those faults, they will leave me." This fear keeps agoraphobics motivated to please others and to live up to their perfectionistic expectations, while they ignore the signals of exhaustion their bodies are sending them.

STRESS OVERLOAD

One day, finally, the cup of life stresses is filled to overflowing. Our habit is to deny the stress, so we really have no choice but to take it *all* on and add more stress to the already overflowing cup. In Ann's case, she had just moved to a strange city, had taken on the care and nurture of stepchildren and was simultaneously trying to adjust to a year-old marriage. (For others, the birth of a baby, an illness, leaving home for the first time or a job change can precipitate the onset of agoraphobia.) Ann describes her situation: "Intellectually, I knew what I was up against; but once again, I felt that any 'normal' person *should* be able to handle the load with grace and aplomb. I stayed frustrated with myself and with the fact that I didn't feel 'good' or 'on top of the situation.' I didn't sleep well. I had headaches. I wanted to give up. But giving up meant failure, and failure meant criticism—from others *and* from myself. On and on I went until, one day, I had the panic attack that got my attention. First, I felt a bit antsy; then I noticed that my neck was stiff. Immediately, the inside of my mouth began to dry up as I started to realize what was coming. Looking around frantically for a bathroom, I became aware that breathing and swallowing were getting more and more difficult. Then the awful numbness in my hands and feet began, paralyzing me and preventing escape. I was scared to death."

Naturally, as intellectualizers, we think that our first panic attack has a message attached to it, but we assume that the message is impending death or lunacy. The actual message is that we have overburdened ourselves. Suppose that Ann had understood about stress and stress overloads; suppose she had understood that a good rest was in order so that her problems would not appear so overwhelming; suppose she had known that nothing bizarre or unusual had occurred; suppose she had recognized that many other people had felt the same way. Just think how she might have reacted if only she had known what was happening *and* that it was sensible and logical and could be used constructively to alter her habits. She says: "I firmly believe that if I had understood the message my body was trying to give me, I would never have experienced the second in a long succession of panic attacks."

THE CULMINATION: AGORAPHOBIA

Because we are unable to put fears to rest, we find that the second panic attack pulls the rug right out from under us. Added to our burgeoning life stresses is another, more emotionally depleting stress: the fear that panic lurks around every corner. We are always on guard. We use more and more of our energy in anticipating the inevitable, and though we are seldom surprised by panic, we are always unaccustomed to the paralyzing fear we feel. We find ourselves in a spiral of fear—stress—fear—stress, and the merry-go-round won't stop.

Making the connection between your personality traits and the agoraphobic syndrome of fear is important. Look over the following chart to conceptualize your development of the agoraphobic condition.

You came into this world with these GIFTS:

SENSITIVITY • CREATIVE INTELLIGENCE
OPENNESS

As a child, you probably experienced:

Instability/Alcoholism • Critical Rearing
Emotional Repression
Fear of Mental Illness • Separation Anxiety

The adult you have become is characterized by:

The need to be in CONTROL • Fear of Rejection/Judgment
Perfectionism • Intellectualizing/Worrying • Dependability

Enter:

STRESS OVERLOAD

PANIC

PANIC

PANIC

PANIC

PANIC

AGORAPHOBIA
The Learned Anxiety Reaction

Here you are now:

FEARFUL

LIMITED

*   *   *

There are several things to remember from this chapter:

1) It is important to know why you developed agoraphobia only so that you can stop frightening yourself about what may have caused it and what may be going on.

2) Your inborn traits include intelligence and sensitivity. These predispose you to react strongly to environmental stressors.

3) You were reared in a certain milieu, usually with separation anxiety, chaos, rigid rules, worries and without the freedom to express a healthy range of feelings.

4) You developed into a perfectionistic adult, very conscious of how you appear to others and of how you are performing.

5) At a time of stress in your life, you began to have symptoms of tension and anxiety. These symptoms went unexplained and, after a time, became a learned and chronic anxiety reaction. This frightened you and began to limit your life as you attempted to deal with the feelings by avoiding places or people that you felt brought them on or worsened them.

4

What Is Normal?

EVERY FEELING we might experience when anxiety strikes is a very familiar and normal feeling when we put it in the proper context. It seems that *all* of us who become frightened by anxiety are baffled about the whys and wherefores of our own body's reactions. Even though it has happened many times, it always comes as a surprise to the two of us when a trained medical professional begins treatment in our CHAANGE program. Doctors, biologists, nurses, physical therapists and counselors are knowledgeable about the mechanisms of *other* people's bodies, but can easily have trouble understanding and accepting what is going on with their *own*.

Let's take a look at what happens in our bodies when we are stimulated or aroused. Imagine for a moment that you are perched at the very top of a roller-coaster ride. The descent lies before you, and you are already anticipating what you will feel as you go whooshing down to the bottom. Your heart is pounding away in anticipation; you are gripping the restraining bar with slippery hands, and there is a knot the size of a watermelon in the pit of your stomach. Are you surprised by these feelings? No; we expect to feel adrenaline coursing through our system when we set out to excite ourselves. However, if these same feelings occur for no obvious reason, we don't recognize them as a normal reaction to arousal; instead, we become convinced that we have never felt that way before and we must be suffering from some catastrophic disease.

Remember that we grew up very desirous of being in control. We kept that control in place by denying our body's reactions and pushing ahead, driven by our need for approval. "If I ignore this headache, it will probably go away." "So, I'm tired; all I need is some coffee and I can put in a few more hours." Perhaps we even take some pleasure in our ability to keep on long after others would have stopped; but it is a perverse pleasure that soon backfires.

This sort of habitual need to control can cause us to repress all our other feelings. We hold back tears even when we feel a desperate need to cry. We hardly ever laugh to the point of hysteria for fear of appearing foolish. We miss the exquisite tingle of an embrace because we are busy checking out our emotions and worrying what others might think. We hold in our anger and run from confrontations because our bodies might betray us and cause our hands to shake and our voices to quaver. It's not that we don't know that these feelings exist; it's more that we have learned to be emotional bystanders.

This behavior is our undoing when stress occurs. Were we not so consumed by the need to be in control and to appear competent, we would be able to recognize stress and then understand that we can't possibly govern everything. Faison remembers: "Not long before I went away to college, I had two lingering illnesses, one a result of the other. Nevertheless, I pushed myself to get prepared for school. I was the oldest child in our family and the first to leave the nest, so the additional pressure of my family's expectations was overwhelming. I truly felt that it was up to me to perform in a way that would heap pride upon Mother, Daddy, my sister, brother and grandparents. No one bothered to mention, nor did I realize, that the first day away from familiar surroundings and friends would be scary and lonely. The emotional strain of the weeks preceding my entrance into a new world, coupled with my tired and weakened body, was ample stress to produce a doozy of a panic attack."

The body reactions that accompany panic cannot be denied. Since we can't ignore them, we begin to lie in wait for them to happen. Every symptom becomes exaggerated to the point that to describe it would be to underrate it. Sweat is not sweat; it is water pouring from our bodies. A racing heart doesn't just pound; it fairly shakes the rib cage. Numbness becomes paralysis. A dry mouth cannot open. Hyperventilation doesn't shorten our breath; it literally stops it. The control we valued so much has disappeared, and our very bodies, or so it seems, are killing us.

We become so afraid of our body's reactions that we hold *back* and hold *on* even more than before. We refrain from anything that might bring about any symptom and deny, deny, deny. We have forgotten what a roller coaster feels like, so we fail to make important connections. The connections are there, though, and we will begin to see them when we begin to relax and learn.

Our bodies are really marvelous machines which have been given to us to enjoy and use. The signals our bodies produce are clear and informational, and we have a responsibility to ourselves to use this information. Your body's messages are unique to you. Faison knows when she is tired because she gets dull headaches. Ann says her tired signal is a stiffness in her shoulders and a feeling of confusion. Some people feel irritable when tired, while others report feeling achy all over. No matter whether it's one symptom or a combination of symptoms, your body does send you a signal that says, "Stop, I am worn out." Our job is to heed that signal and consciously make the effort to stop.

We are not suggesting that it is necessary for us to focus so closely on our bodies that we become too introspective, but body cues do provide us with needed information about ourselves. By listening, heeding and readjusting to our early warning messages, not only do we *feel* more in charge of our lives, we actually *are* more in charge.

Having a clear picture of the physiological changes that occur when adrenaline is introduced into the bloodstream will help in demythicizing panicky feelings. The moment the brain sends the body a "fear" message, the adrenal glands get busy. With the very first flash of danger, we feel a remarkably increased awareness. Our bodies can tingle all over and our eyes widen, seeking out the menacing intruder. Our body is either getting ready to run away or preparing itself for an unwanted blow. Blood rushes from the extremities and pools around vital organs (stomach, lungs and heart). This rapid blood movement brings about some distressful sensations like dizziness, light-headedness, numbness in the extremities, dry mouth, inability to focus well, a desire to relieve both bladder and bowels, and upset stomach. Often we become so aware of our breathing that we overbreathe, or hyperventilate; our hearts may race as we gulp for air.

The adrenaline reaction is an adaptive mechanism in humans, and is probably one of the most important functions we have developed. It was meant to focus our attention and our energies. As a species, we probably would not have survived without it.

What about the person who never really has a full-blown panic attack, but always feels uneasy and anxious? Instead of being given booming physiological messages, his body is more or less "oozing" just enough adrenaline into his system to produce an "on guard" feeling. Often, with this kind of anxiety, no avoidance behaviors actually develop, but every accomplishment seems to have been a chore. Once again, we are talking about too many pressures with too few appropriate coping skills, rather than an innate weakness of character. The remedy for both chronic anxiety and anxiety coupled with panic is exactly the same.

Agoraphobia is a phenomenon of young adulthood. During those years, we tend to be self-conscious about our bodies, and because we are intellectualizers, we fundamentally distrust and dislike all that "body business" anyway.

Operating under the assumption that we are "ill," most of us will go to great lengths to have our malfunctioning bodies examined thoroughly.

Faison describes her first experience with agoraphobia: "I was knocked off my feet by my first panic episode. Not only was I not expecting it, I didn't even know what had hit me. In 1966, newly graduated from high school, I was eager in a guarded way about going off to college in the fall. There was no discussion about *whether* I would go to college—I just knew I would go. The college I chose had a large campus, and was the same one that both my mother and grandmother had attended.

"All during the summer after graduation, I felt 'funny.' I had trouble sleeping; I felt on edge, jumpy and exhausted most of the time. I had two jobs that summer, and I had not completely recovered my energy and pep after a long, difficult bout with the mumps and the complications that accompanied my illness. Yet all summer long, I never let up on myself. I went out every night, ate a lot of junk food and drank a great many Cokes. I began smoking cigarettes. I did not allow myself to rest or to consider what lay ahead of me. I refused to deal with my confused emotions as I anticipated leaving home. Whenever I thought about going to college, I would almost get nauseated. A little jolt of fear would course through my body and I would direct my thoughts elsewhere. I did not know the importance of facing those fears head on, and did not realize it would help to talk with someone who could reassure me that my feelings were absolutely normal. I also did not associate my insomnia and other symptoms with my physical and emotional stress, so

I never did a thing except wonder why I was feeling this way.

"Not long after my parents had unloaded my belongings and said their goodbyes, the dizziness began. Without letting up, it quickly led into shaking, heart palpitations, confusion and finally hyperventilation. Within the space of two or three minutes, I found myself falling apart. My first thought was that I was having a stroke, and as soon as I thought that, there were sensations to suggest that my diagnosis was correct. I began to see black spots in front of my eyes and to sense numbness in my arms and hands. By now, I was frantic and knew that I had to get medical help right away.

"It took a few minutes for me to be able to stand and walk well enough to get to the infirmary. It seemed a long way from the dormitory, and it was. I know exactly how far because I made the trip dozens and dozens of times during the course of that dreadful year. This first visit was to set the stage for all subsequent visits. I announced myself to the nurse behind the appointment register and told her how close I was to dying at that very moment. She told me to sit down and wait. I waited. By the time I was called in to see the doctor, I was through with the worst of my 'stroke' and was feeling only those shaky aftermath feelings of panic. But my memory was good, and I was able to describe, in detail, what had befallen me and how important it was that I be given some medication immediately to 'cure' whatever was wrong with me.

"I know that the poor, patient doctor must have heard this particular lament a thousand times or more. She went to work examining for physical causes: checking my blood pressure, looking in my ears, taking my temperature, taking a blood sample. Finally, the verdict was in: there was nothing wrong, nothing whatsoever. Very sadly, I walked back to the dorm, still feeling shaky and nervous. Something *was* wrong, I knew it was. It isn't normal to feel this way. I think she's missed something. What if I am really dying? What if I pass out right now? What if I *never* feel any different than I am feeling at this moment? I was scared to death and I didn't know where to turn.

"Over the next few months, the attacks of panic and the periods of chronic anxiety stayed with me like a shadow. I began to be a regular at the infirmary—they all knew me, and I feared they thought that I was a crazy person. Each day I felt a little more despair at the thought that I would never find the solution to this puzzle, yet every day I had hope that the end of this suffering would be near. I was not going to classes much. Some I never attended, not even showing up for scheduled tests and exams. For instance, I just didn't go to my biology lab at all. It was out of the question that I could sit *anywhere* for three hours with the anxiety and agitation that I was feeling, so I gave up trying. Likewise, college algebra was out of the question because that class met for an hour and a half twice a week.

"After several successive weeks of very hypochondriacal behavior, I once again presented myself at the infirmary and was seen by the one male doctor on the staff. He was a lovely, kind man, and I had great hopes that he would take pity on me and devote himself to 'finding out' what was wrong with me. Instead, I was devastated to have him tell me that he was referring me to the school psychiatrist. I was stunned. I was not having strokes or cardiac problems after all. I did not have an obscure inner-ear disease. I was mentally ill, and there was no hope for me.

"Over the next thirteen years, I *did* see a number of psychiatrists, but I sought out all sorts of other specialists as well. Because the symptoms of agoraphobia are physical (often mimicking those of other illnesses and conditions that have medical explanations), it is not surprising that we are constantly seeking a medical diagnosis and treatment. Throughout the years of my condition, I visited about thirty doctors and underwent tests of every description and duration, from blood work to electroencephalograms (EEGs). Either the doctors were overlooking a sinister malignant tumor somewhere, or the disease I was suffering from was so rare that diagnosis was impossible. Did I ever connect my symptoms with what was going on in my life that first day of panic? No! My compulsive and lengthy search was for the answer to a riddle that somebody else would have to solve."

ANXIETY MEDICATIONS

Though neither of us was ever convinced that our physicians knew what was truly wrong with us, each of us was prescribed anxiety medications. Faison says that even though she hated the thought of becoming drug-dependent, she would have swallowed a moon rock if it promised an answer. Her answer, however, did *not* come in pill form. In light of today's expanded understanding of the relationship between the biological, psychological and stress-related aspects of the anxiety condition, it is possible to take a realistic look at discoveries about the effectiveness of certain medications that can, if properly administered, help, not hinder, your learning process. Each person is unique; the proper decision about medication to support your learning must be based on what will be most helpful for *you*.

Supportive medications offer advantages for some, and also potential disadvantages. These must be weighed, each against the other. Ideally, a prescription medication should help a person regain a sense of equilibrium so that other forms of learning can take place. Although exclusive reliance on medication may "work" for some individuals, we find that the majority of agoraphobics desire to become less drug-reliant and eventually drug-free. We feel encouraged by the increase in the proper investigation of these medications. However, we *do* feel that each person needs to make an *informed* decision about this, together with a physician, in order to determine a sensible course. We encourage you to ask your physician questions about medications and how they can be used to *support* this learning process.

DISORDERS OF CHANCE

There are several physiological conditions that have the same symptoms as the anxiety reaction, and you should have a complete medical examination to rule out any physical causes for your symptoms.

1. MITRAL-VALVE PROLAPSE

This condition has received attention from some professionals who theorized that it was a contributing factor in agoraphobia. Mitral-valve prolapse (often called "heart murmur") is a relatively harmless valve malformation in the upper chamber of the heart. Those who have been diagnosed as having this condition report various symptoms, such as rapid heartbeat, mild chest pain or skipped heartbeats. Ann's family discovered that she had this condition when she was about five, but because there was never any emphasis placed upon it, she never worried about it. As a matter of fact, Ann had recovered completely from agoraphobia before any suggestion of a possible connection between the two conditions was made. We both feel that had she focused on the heart condition, she could easily have confused the symptoms and slowed her recovery. Many people have mitral-valve prolapse; only a small percentage frighten themselves with the condition.

The latest research indicates that about 15 percent of agoraphobics have this benign heart condition—the same percentage as is found in the population at large. There are no other clinical differences between agoraphobics who have MVP and those who do not, according to research; the presence or absence of MVP need not have an effect on agoraphobia treatment. A physical examination will readily disclose the condition, if it exists.

A young woman from Texas, who is a perfect example of the confusion that can result from a mild condition such as MVP, comes to mind. She was taking our program "in home," using our literature and taped sessions. She was highly anxious and worried, to the point that she frequently called our counselors to receive reassurance. Having heard about MVP, she rushed off to her physician, insisting that he conduct a thorough examination. Conscious of her concerns, her doctor reluctantly told her that she did have this condition. He went on to say that he wished he hadn't had to tell her, because the worst thing about MVP was the intense worry it was likely to produce in her mind. We worked with her for many months to help her get to the point where she could let go of her nonproductive worry about her health and get on with the business of living a happy life.

2. HYPOGLYCEMIA

Hypoglycemia (low blood sugar) sends body signals similar to those produced by acute anxiety. Light-headedness, shaky hands, wobbly legs and a feeling of confusion can be indicative of this condition. Low blood sugar can easily be treated by close attention to diet and health habits. As slow-burning sugars (complex carbohydrates) and proteins are introduced in place of speedy boosters (simple sugars) several times each day, the symptoms of hypoglycemia diminish. A glucose-tolerance test will diagnose this condition. Agoraphobia and hypoglycemia can occur simultaneously, and both can be alleviated.

3. MENIÈRE'S SYNDROME

This inner-ear dysfunction received heavy press some years ago, as did mitral-valve prolapse. Although the symptoms of Menière's syndrome include dizziness and a ringing in the ears, not all agoraphobia sufferers experience those as primary symptoms.

4. WOMEN'S CONCERNS

Women have a couple of special issues that create anxious feelings. Not all women suffer from premenstrual syndrome (PMS), but all female bodies do go through monthly hormonal (chemical) changes during the years of menstruation. A woman's body is designed for childbearing. The physiological changes that occur during these thirty or more years are a bonus rather than a curse. Puberty, and the emotional upheaval associated with it, prepares for pregnancy. The natural chemical changes during pregnancy protect both mother and child. The discomfort of menopause is a short-lived experience in view of what it represents.

The predictable rise and fall of hormone levels (adrenaline included) can be felt emotionally, physically and, sometimes, both ways. There are indeed physiological symptoms that can normally be present when you begin to menstruate and when you cease to menstruate; headaches, depression, hot flashes, heart palpitations are just a few. None should be fear-producing when we understand and accept them.

Most agoraphobics make the mistake of thinking that diagnosis of a specific physical disorder will explain all anxiety symptoms. It's easy to fall into the trap of believing "I am going to be stuck with this all of my life," never understanding that one can, in fact, learn to play a major role in one's own recovery.

DISORDERS OF CHOICE

While there are some physiological disorders over whose cause we have no control, there are others that we cause to happen.

CAFFEINE

Anything containing caffeine (coffee, tea, soft drinks and some over-the-counter medicines, for example) produces arousal symptoms: shaky hands, rapid heartbeat, profuse sweating, edginess and on and on. Caffeine is a significant stimulant, and it is one that we rarely consider as we try to discover the cause of our tension and ways to alleviate our anxiety. As an acute-anxiety or agoraphobia sufferer, you are extrasensitive to all stimuli, and should avoid caffeine as much as possible.

NICOTINE

Nicotine produces a zing to the senses in the same way adrenaline does, so you need to be aware that your numb fingers can be a result of smoking rather than the first sign of an anxiety attack. If you continue with this habit, you will constantly have to deal with the side effects of nicotine and the physical symptoms it produces.

Faison didn't think she could face the stress of stopping her smoking habit while she was battling anxiety, but had to daily face the fact that she was increasing her anxiety levels by puffing away on cigarettes. Although it may seem that taking a puff of a cigarette calms the spirit, the reverse is true. Faison can still see herself struggling alone at the wheel of her car, gulping for air and lighting up. The more she inhaled the tobacco smoke, the less good air her heaving lungs received. Now she—and Ann—know that smoking only makes you feel worse, not better.

ALCOHOL

How many people do you suppose drink to quell anxieties? Probably most habitual drinkers do so to dull or inhibit the pain of life, and certainly anxiety is one of life's biggest pains. Alcohol is a depressant; we often assume that a couple of drinks will calm us down and curb some of our fears. Many of us, however, understand the perils of alcoholism from our early-childhood experiences. The two of us reacted so differently toward drinking that an explanation of our extremes might be helpful to you.

Ann and Earl usually had a drink together in the early evening after he got home from the office. One drink would lead to two, and she would begin to forget her anxieties and feel hungry for a hefty dinner. She always seemed to feel better at the end of the day, but worried that she was turning more and more to alcohol for help in coping. For her, the need for relief outweighed the worry, so she continued to have cocktails while wondering if she was walking down the path toward alcoholism.

Faison, on the other hand, shied away from any alcoholic intake whatsoever. There were two fears that kept her abstinent. One was that *any* amount of whiskey (even in desserts) would cause violent physical reactions that she couldn't control. The other was the fear that she might like the effect of alcohol and become an alcoholic. Neither of us had a mature approach to alcohol, and we spent a great deal of energy worrying about its possible control of our lives. Had we been able to separate our desire or lack of desire for alcohol from our anxiety condition, we probably would have made much better decisions for ourselves. Your choice in this matter is best if judiciously based on your beliefs and your intelligent understanding of what drinking does and does not do. Using a drink to halt the anxiety reaction only creates additional problems. Problems are also created by being obsessively fearful of the physical reactions to the small amount of rum in a piece of cake.

NUTRITION

It goes without saying that a balanced diet helps you to be healthy. Some people have reported that the stress for them at the onset of their panic was a crash diet or having eaten poorly over a period of months. Sugar produces a metabolic "rush" while it briefly raises your energy level; it also produces a "crash" when the rush is over. Anxiety symptoms can result not only from overeating, but also from undereating.

Now that you have a clearer picture of what is happening in your body during an anxiety reaction, you can begin to cast off a lot of the fear that has been associated with those reactions. All of us have a tendency to overreact to physical symptoms, but as you develop a realistic understanding of the workings of your body, you will be increasingly able to make better choices for yourself.

*   *   *

This is an important chapter. We hope that you will leave it with new information which offers you a sense of understanding and relief:

1) The body's reaction to panic and anxiety is a normal, understandable human adaptive mechanism which can be thought of as productive and useful. Since it is not inherently frightening, you can learn to view it in a nonfrightened manner.

2) Stress is an inevitable aspect of human existence; all persons react in some way to times of stress. Because of your intelligence and supersensitivity, your perfectionism and your need for control, you have come to react to such times with anxiety.

3) Almost all of us who have suffered with panic anxiety have been through years of fear, searching for an answer and a doctor to help us. During these years, our lives, understandably, have centered around our worries and concerns that we may be dying, having heart attacks or, somehow, losing our minds. We are not. Now that you understand adrenaline and the bodily symptoms it produces (heart palpitations, hyperventilation, sweating, shakiness, confusion, tingling, swaying sensations and so on), you can start practicing not frightening yourself with these responses.

4) When considering where to begin treatment, assess possible physical problems that may mimic or inten-

sify anxiety. When considering medication therapy, review and decide (with the assistance of your physician) which avenues are best for *you*.

5) Remember that agoraphobia is a learned condition even though the predisposition or tendency toward its development is inherited. This does not mean that you can't overcome agoraphobia, any more than people can't overcome ulcers or headaches. We did, and you most certainly can.

5

▼▼▼▼▼▼▼

Familiar Avoidances

▲▲▲▲▲▲▲▲

AVOIDANCE IS a "Catch-22." We avoid in the hope of quelling anxiety and end up feeling twice as anxious because of the avoidance. There are thousands of everyday examples of avoidance behavior that have nothing to do with agoraphobia. How many times have you said or heard someone else say that she really works her best under pressure? What we are really doing is rationalizing the fact that we have put off a task until the last minute because we don't want to do it, probably because we don't think we will perform it as well as we should. The longer we put off the task because of this fear of failure or fear of judgment, the more anxious we become. Finally, at the eleventh hour, we scramble around frantically, and usually end up feeling disappointed about the mistakes we made in our haste, rather than feeling relieved and proud of a job well done. It is certainly possible that those of us who grew up with a strong need to be thought of as capable and competent exhibit this behavior more than others. However, avoidance behavior patterns are *not* unique to the agoraphobic; we are just *better* at it!

We agoraphobics turn an "I don't want to" into an "I can't" in a hurry. There is a realm of difference between not wanting to do something and not being *able* to do something, which is exactly what "I can't" connotes. Those first few episodes of panic convinced Ann (1) that she should not be *trusted* to drive, and (2) that she had somehow lost her *ability* to drive. She says: "I believed that if I were to get into my car and strike out on my own, the world would end for me right then and there. I had been a licensed driver for half my life, I had never had an accident, I had taught two teenagers to drive and I considered myself a good and cautious driver. Up until my first anxiety attack, I had enjoyed driving, but none of that mattered because suddenly I was too scared to drive. I avoided the fear by saying and believing, 'I can't.' Did this new belief of mine cure my anxiety about driving? No. What if the school called to say that one of my children needed me? Would I be able to say 'I can't' to that? Just knowing that my car was sitting idly in the garage made me anxious, because it reminded me that there was so much I *could* be doing if I *could* drive. Thinking about my newly developed incapacity brought on just about as many fear symptoms as had rocked me in the car, and only reinforced my belief in 'I can't.' "

A good number of agoraphobics avoid nothing, and just complain that they feel anxious and uncomfortable in varied situations and events. A larger percentage of sufferers are like Ann in that they develop a system of avoidances, hoping to control the fear symptoms. A small number of agoraphobics allow their avoidance system to overwhelm them to the extent that they become "housebound." They begin innocently enough, by merely trying their best to feel as O.K. as possible under the circumstances. Ann focused on the fact that she had been *alone* in the car when panic first struck and *alone* the second time; therefore, her system of avoidances centered around being by herself. Before she realized what was happening, she was saying "I can't shop alone, I can't walk down the street alone, I can't do anything without a familiar and understanding person literally pressed beside me." She knew she was in trouble when she began to say "I can't stay home alone." It was at that point that she knew the avoidance system wasn't doing what it was supposed to do, and that she would have to get help.

The avoidance system of behaviors can work for the fellow who has a fear of snakes and lives in New York City because there is a good chance that he is never going to encounter a snake. Avoidances don't work for agoraphobics because we are constantly confronted with what we fear most: our own minds and bodies.

As you read this, you are thinking that we may be able to understand some *other* agoraphobic's doubts and fears, but that yours are truly different and that you will unquestionably be the person who *does* drop dead from panic, or whose thoughts finally *do* succeed in driving him crazy. You are also thinking that we are never going to describe your particular physical symptoms; therefore, we can't possibly understand why you have to avoid. We may not hit your symptoms right on the nose, but that doesn't mean that we haven't felt what you are feeling. During the past eight years we have talked with thousands of anxiety victims, and never once have we been surprised or alarmed by detailed descriptions. We are purposely *not* filling these pages with physical and mental symptoms because (a) we still might not talk specifically about yours and you would then be *certain* that you were different and (b) you would pick up on everyone else's symptoms, and we think you probably have enough to deal with already.

After the first few episodes of panic have occurred, a remarkable thing takes place that leads agoraphobics to believe that there is a massive attack somewhere in the future that will absolutely destroy them. We call this "fine-tuning the panic reaction."

Though there are literally hundreds of anxiety or adrenaline reactions, after the first few attacks the ones that we repeat are those which frighten us the most. Not too long after Ann's second panic attack, she says she began to focus on three symptoms: dry mouth, inability to focus her eyes and numbness, as well as a symptom which always indicated that an attack was forthcoming: lots of trips to the bathroom. These symptoms accompanied every succeeding attack. No matter how uncomfortable it may be, it would be helpful if you took a good look at your physical symptoms of panic, and thought carefully about just why they scare you to such an extent. Ann tells this story that should give you insight into how sensitive we are to our own bodies; how suggestible we can be to another person's distress; how avoidance can hurt more than help:

"Several years ago, I went on a sailing trip with Earl and two very good friends of ours. This was Diana and Sam's first sailing trip without a hired captain, and I certainly wanted to prove that I was an excellent second mate, as well as a fearless sailor. The week we picked for sailing in the Bahamas could not have been worse, weatherwise; it was rainy and cold, and by midweek the winds had picked up to a consistent thirty-five knots, blowing night and day. By Thursday, we decided to sail to a resort port and languish on dry land.

"We sailed for hours against a roaring wind with our old boat groaning into the waves. Suddenly, we hit bottom with a giant crash and were stuck hard aground. At first it didn't seem so bad, except for the loud banging and thumping. But soon it occurred to me that Diana was feeling apprehensive about our predicament, suggesting to me that *I* should feel scared too. First, I felt nauseated, though I have never been seasick in my life. Next, I felt my hands and feet begin to grow numb. I was so busy being scared that I couldn't open my mouth to speak, so naturally Diana assumed that something horrifying was happening to me, and *she* became concerned. The more concerned she got, the more I panicked, until I had finally succeeded in impeding the flow of blood to my arms and hands and they became a dark and ominous blue. (I had on socks and shoes, so no one will ever know what color my feet had turned!)

"Finally, Earl got tired of all the dramatics belowdecks while he and Sam were fighting the elements up top, so he simply demanded that we come up and join the effort. Weakly, I climbed the ladder, and I immediately discovered how ridiculously I had been behaving. We were in no danger at all. The boat was aground, and being aground meant that we were perhaps in five feet of water, at most. The shoreline was less than fifty yards away. In fact, several people were standing on the beach waving at us. Any of us could have climbed off our boat, paddled about ten feet and then *walked* to shore! I had to admit to myself that all my spectacular symptoms had been for naught. I also had to realize that I was capable of taking one little symptom of anxiety and blowing enough fear into it to create those pitiful-looking arms and hands. I decided right then and there never to do that again. I had perceived a danger where none existed, and I had systematically brought about a panic attack simply because I knew how to do it so well. I wore myself *and* Diana out with unnecessary alarm for several hours, when one minute's rational assessment of the situation would have been quite enough to end my fears.''

We want you to begin to see how much energy it takes to try to avoid the inevitable, and that reality is often far less frightening than the assumptions we have allowed fear to dictate. During that sailing trip, Ann reacted out of habit to a *perceived* danger. She had learned over and over again to react to fear by producing physical symptoms, and had honed those symptoms to their scariest. Nonproductive, fear-enhancing habits kept her from climbing up on deck and taking a good look around. Panic had become her habitual reaction to fear, and avoidance her habitual reaction to panic. These habits are meant to be broken, and we are going to do that by replacing them with behaviors and habits that will serve you much better.

Faison used a tip from Dr. Claire Weekes to deal with her fear of taking risks, specifically the risk of having a panic attack while doing something new or frightening. Dr. Weekes uses the metaphor of "Grandma's muffins." She says that the unmistakable aroma of muffins baking had always transported her to her grandmother's house in her memory, no matter where she was or how many years had passed since she had last actually been there. She recalls: "This helped me stop my panic many times. For example, I might bravely decide to take a trip. I would pack my suitcase and take the car to the service station to be filled with gas, having made careful plans that I could not easily get out of. The day would arrive and there I would be, driving down the highway, bound for another city, usually traveling along rural, wooded roads. Predictably, at some point, I would begin to feel anxious. My mind would automatically react with 'Oh, no! Why did I feel that?' Then I'd call on my new learning and say 'Oh, I know, it's just like Grandma's muffins—it's habit.'" The sights and sounds and smells of places and things bring back the emotions associated with those things. We accept and appreciate the fact when we consider the lovely and reassuring things in life (like Grandma's muffins), but often we forget that uncomfortable memories are conjured up in precisely the same way.

We thought you might like to take a look at how CHAANGE participants rank their avoidances and comfort levels as they enter our program. Some examples in the list of avoidances were provided by Mathews, Gelder and Johnson from their book *Agoraphobia: Nature and Treatment*. Were Ann to have filled this out during her agoraphobic years, she would have added the word "alone" after each example and then thrown in a few specifics of her own at the bottom. Stop for a minute and take a look at your avoidances, using this scale.

Situation/Event	Frequency of Avoidance of Situation					Level of Discomfort in Situation				
	never avoid	seldom avoid	sometimes avoid	often avoid	always avoid	comfortable	slightly uncomfortable	uncomfortable	very uncomfortable	panicky
Example: Standing in line				√					√	
Driving										
Shopping malls										
Church/Synagogue										
Grocery stores										
Being in crowds										
Flying										
Traveling alone by bus										
Walking alone on busy streets										
Going into crowded shops or stores										
Going alone far from home										
Large open spaces										
Add others below if appropriate:										

*   *   *

Listed below are several concepts that we want you to have
learned from this chapter:

1) We all (every human being) avoid situations and
   events to protect ourselves from something. That
   something could be as simple as boredom or as complex as the fear of rejection; nevertheless, avoidance
   is really a protective device.
2) Agoraphobics avoid in an effort to minimize anxiety.
3) Making a rational assessment of a situation diminishes
   the intensity of your reaction to it.

Angry?

ANGER and anxiety go hand in hand, and *we* believe that anger is a singularly important issue in the agoraphobic condition. Our Random House Dictionary defines anger as: "a strong feeling of displeasure and belligerence aroused by a real or supposed wrong." We are all truly wronged from time to time. We all get angry, and we all have a need to ventilate our anger. It really is O.K. to *get* angry, to *act* angry and to *say* you're angry, as long as you are clear about *what* has made you angry.

We are betting that you are mad that you have agoraphobia. Not only are you furious at the condition, but you also hate yourself for having developed it. When you are not angry and hating yourself, you are feeling sorry for yourself, which then leads to your being even angrier than before. You feel that you have been robbed of your dignity, and way down deep you sense that you may have brought all of this on yourself, and therefore you may feel justified in hating yourself.

Lesson one in dealing productively with anger is to clearly identify what is wrong, why it is wrong and what can be done to change the wrong to right. Saving up injustices to stew about late in the night doesn't change anything or make us feel one bit better. Having a screaming fit might relieve a little tension, but it will never clear the air or solve the problem.

Ann talks about coming to terms with anger: "I could take you all the way back to my childhood and show you that I never could deal with angry feelings; but it would be better to concentrate on the angers and frustrations in my life just prior to my first panic attack.

"When I married Earl, I viewed myself as the champion of his causes. I would forsake all others and start from scratch with this wonderfully handsome and intelligent man, welcoming his poor, mistreated children into my well-managed home.

"Was I a wee bit angry when life didn't follow my paint-by-numbers outline? Starting from scratch turned out to mean just that. Earl's ex-wife kept all of his furniture, my ex-husband had all of mine and we couldn't exactly sit on romance, or eat at the table of undying love. And this was in Gainesville, Georgia, the Chicken Capital of the World, where every day at noon the weatherman reported the temperature, the chance of showers and the chicken-feather density in the atmosphere.

"But love did conquer much for us. We built our little house in the trees, the children and I made some necessary compromises and I began to enjoy Gainesville, thinking that life was just going to be O.K. We had one year of peace and then, slap, out came the rug from beneath our feet and we were off to Rockford to start over once again. I was afraid that if I balked and said 'No' to Earl I might be faced with another failed marriage and guilt over my inability to keep a relationship glued together. With teeth clenched, I agreed to move.

"I hated Rockford, I hated our house, I hated Earl, I hated his ex-wife for dumping two more children on me, I hated my ex-husband for not having loved me enough and I blamed them one and all for my misery. I acted like a martyr much of the time, and I often flew off the handle at insignificant things, but I never openly acknowledged to myself or to anyone else the rage inside me. Often I would catch a glimpse of those angers and push them right back inside, fearing that if I got really mad and said so, I would appear foolish and childish.

"For months I kept myself going by thinking how courageously I was behaving in the face of all our troubles, until finally the pressure became too great. Those pent-up angry feelings led me to anxiety and then on to depression. I felt depressed about feeling anxious, and I felt anxious about feeling so angry, and then I got angrier at myself for feeling anxious and depressed!

"My typical behavior was to lash out at the person I believed most responsible for my pain. For instance, Earl would come home late from work. I would read him the riot act for holding up dinner, and then I would be off and running, bringing up every old injury I could think of. God knows, if I had been he, I would have turned on my heel and walked back out the door; but good old Earl would patiently wait for the storm to die down, then calmly ask, 'Are you finished?' This would inevitably send me into another hysterical tirade.

"I would have been a lot more effective with Earl, and I would have been able to give up my anger sooner had I: *stopped* (relaxed both mind and body); *identified the anger* (I am mad at Earl because I don't know where he is and it is not like him to be late without calling and that scares me); *stuck to the issue* (I am mad at Earl only for being late today and I don't want him to make a habit of this; he won't hear me if I insist on dumping extraneous pet peeves on top of this hurt); *stated my position* ('Earl, I feel really angry about your being late. You know that I worry when I don't know where you are'). Instead, my inappropriate response created a smoke screen and did nothing to resolve the real problem."

This four-step alternative of *stop, identify, clarify, state your position* will work for you *every time*. You may not always be right, but you will have given yourself and the person with whom you are angry the best possible chance at a productive reconciliation. And that is what we are after: a chance to reconcile our differences so that the hurts aren't getting in the way of our happiness.

Angers that we hold in check, that we repress or choose not to deal with for one reason or another, tend to stockpile. It is because they are not resolved that we pull them out every now and then to stew over them, rekindle them and magnify them. Unless we rid ourselves of this collection of old angers, there is no alternative for us but to feel anxious and/or depressed.

Before we show you how to reduce your stockpile of angers, we think we had better stop and talk about depression and what it does to us. There are basically two kinds of depression. Biochemical depression is inherited and clinically treatable with drug therapy. The other type of depression is situational and reactive. To put it simply, we feel overwhelmed and angry about our life stresses and become despondent about our inability to correct the situation.

Depression, like anxiety, is a stress in itself and is manifested by such symptoms as inadequate sleep, little or no appetite, fatigue, little interest in sexual contact, a lot of ruminating about the past and a grim outlook. Depression can get in the way of the learning and growth process because it is an energy and motivation robber. Take a careful look at your depression levels, and assess the extent to which you believe this stress is standing in the way of your progress. Contact your physician if you feel that your distress is overwhelming. Asking for and beginning a remedy for depression will enhance this growth process. Both of us found that our levels of depression subsided as we worked on ways to reduce anxiety.

To dump out the bag of old angers that we've carried around for years takes a somewhat different approach from confronting current angers. It is *not* productive to call up your mother and blast her for wrongs that were never righted in your childhood. Neither Mother nor you will feel good after that little waltz down memory lane, and we disagree with anyone who states otherwise. Ann says: "I had a ton of those ancient angers to get rid of myself, but I think that I knew instinctively that I could not change things by opening up old wounds. I had to find a different way to junk my junk. I chose to sit down and have a long talk with myself, taking out each anger, one by one, to examine it for its validity in my life today. As I pulled them out, I became aware that none of them truly had any influence over how things were going for me. I was holding on to them so that I could drag them out and feel sorry for my sweet self every time the world became too much for me to handle; there were times when I actively chose to rub salt into my wounds so that my miseries would justify my statements about life being hard. I found out that those old angers were keeping me anxious, and I decided to let them go. Immediately I could feel how much easier it is for me to cope with one situation at a time, and by allowing those old angers to disappear, I was also free to enjoy relationships with the very people with whom I thought I should be angry.''

A wrong that you incurred twenty years ago, that has no bearing on your present life, that you recall just to wallow in self-pity is absolutely useless to you or to anyone else. It is also useless to resent the fact that life isn't going better for you. We can guarantee you that life won't get any better if all your time is taken up shadowboxing with old hurts. The way you rid yourself of these useless, nonproductive stored-up resentments is not important; it matters only that you do it and that you do it *now*. The energy it takes to stew in your own juices will be much better used in getting on with your life and over your anxieties. We just don't have enough energy to keep the fires of an angry self burning and free ourselves from fear at the same time. The anger and resentment you feel over having to deal with your agoraphobic condition will keep you trapped in that condition, preventing you from taking steps in the right direction.

The method that Ann used to let go of old angers (examining them for any current validity) is not the only way or necessarily the best choice for you. Faison wrote letters. She would sit down at her desk and write a long letter to a person who had caused her pain. She would leave nothing unsaid, detailing events and making sure that she used all the words she felt she had missed the opportunity to say years before. She would read the letter to herself and then carefully tear it into small pieces and throw the whole mess away.

Others who are more physical and athletic than we are have discovered that it can be liberating to identify the persistent anger and then attack it on a tennis court or out at the woodpile. As each tennis ball is tossed aloft, an injustice is imagined, and then—''thwack!''—it's gone. Insults can be chopped, split and neatly stacked for burning.

It is O.K. if you are mad at agoraphobia; just don't make the mistake of being mad at *yourself* for having developed the condition. Let go of being angry at your doctor or your therapist for not being able to help you. Understand that it is not your husband's or wife's fault that you aren't moving out of anxiety. Use our suggested method for dealing with day-to-day angers as you approach your anger at the anxiety condition. *Stop* (relax; there is absolutely nothing physiologically or emotionally wrong with you); *identify the issue* (agoraphobia is what you are dealing with and you know what it is and why you got it); *stick to the issue* (agoraphobia is *all* you have; you are not dying of some unidentifiable malady or rapidly losing your mind) and *state your position* (you will take one step at a time and one day at a time and walk yourself right out of this anxiety). The reason that it is not O.K. for you to be mad at yourself for having developed this condition is that you have neither done anything wrong nor wronged anyone else. The only thing you are guilty of is not allowing yourself to be human and imperfect. If we were perfect and life were perfect, there would be no work left to be done and tomorrow would be just like today, with no challenges and no successes. Accepting our imperfections allows us to realize that anger and anxiety are part of the human condition, and we can decide for ourselves the best ways to deal comfortably with both.

PHYSICAL SYMPTOMS OF ANGER

There is a mind-body connection to be made about angry feelings which will help you in your recovery from agoraphobia. Anger, like fear, produces physical symptoms. Ann describes the first time she made the mind-body connection for herself. She had been living with agoraphobia for about three years and arranging her life around her avoidances: "One morning, I woke to discover that we were completely out of food. All day long I waited for Earl to come home to take me to the store. The more I waited, the angrier I became; the angrier I became, the more physical reactions I experienced.

"As soon as Earl arrived from work, I demanded that he get back into the car and help me with the shopping. Earl declared that he was worn out from his day and just wanted to sit down for a while before venturing out again.

"Before I noticed what I was doing, I jumped into the car and drove down our street and on to the store. I was in aisle three when the reality of the situation hit me. It was right there in the middle of the SaveWay supermarket that I made a very important discovery for myself: I had not been scared or disturbed by heightened physical reactions because I had associated them with the very familiar feelings of anger. They were O.K. because I knew there was a reason for them. The minute I made the connection I got excited, and the more excited I became, the more connections I made.

"The physical symptoms I experienced when I got angry or when I felt excited were exactly the same kinds of symptoms I produced when I panicked. All during my years of agoraphobia I had been putting the wrong label on my physical reactions to anxiety. I had labeled these reactions bizarre, life-threatening and irrational. I had been wrong."

The correct label for physical symptoms that occur with excitement, anger and fear needs only one word to describe what is happening in your body: *arousal*. In every instance your body has been trying to tell you that it was aroused, or "ready," in case you decided to jump for joy, punch out a bad guy or run. Your *body* made no judgments, and it was only your misinterpretation of your body's messages that led you to the assumption that they meant something more. As soon as you apply the correct label to these physical symptoms, you can stop scaring yourself with them. For instance, the minute that you feel the first signs of arousal, you can look at the situation and determine if the physical reactions are required. With panic, our bodies are reacting to a perception of fear rather than an actual danger; therefore, the physical symptoms are a response habit rather than a necessity. Our bodies will calm down quickly when we send a message that says the state of arousal is not required.

Begin to stop frightening yourself by conjuring up how it makes your body feel to be angry, excited or afraid. Think about how very similar these arousal responses are and how very basic and protective they are. Start to give your body calming messages, and recognize the difference between an aroused body and a relaxed body. (We are going to teach you a relaxation technique in Chapter 12, and you may want to skip ahead now and begin practicing this behavior.) There are times when we want to keep our level of arousal high so that we can dance all night or bring an audience to its feet, but there are also times when we need to slow the spin down a bit in order to feel in control. You are the message-giver to your body; it is not the other way around. You can command any feeling you want and any response you need. Practice sending yourself calming messages and you'll see just what we mean. The more you practice, the more automatic these responses will become. Soon you will be able to elicit almost any response you desire by using your own special cue to do so.

*   *   *

In summary, let's look at the important issues we have talked about:

1) Anger is an emotion that we all share, but that few of us learn to deal with productively in our formative years.
2) When confronting current angers: *stop, identify the anger, stick to the issue* and *state your position.*
3) Stockpiled angers produce both anxiety and depression and need to be dumped.
4) Making the mind-body connection between the symptoms of anger and the symptoms of anxiety can help you understand how normal and nonthreatening these body responses are.

Chapter

7

▼▼▼▼▼▼▼

How Your Condition Affects Others

▲▲▲▲▲▲▲▲

AGORAPHOBIA (and the system of behaviors that you have developed because of it) doesn't involve only you. You may have become so concerned about your well-being that you have overlooked what is happening to your family and friends as they react to you. Your agoraphobia affects and involves others when you are married; when you are married with children; when you are raising children without a partner; when you are living with your parents; when you are living with a friend; when you are working with others; even when you are living alone and have no job. The other people in your life have a role to play in your condition and in your recovery from that condition, and you have a responsibility to understand this role.

The CHAANGE treatment program devotes an entire tape session to the family and friends of our participants. We know how difficult it is for a sufferer to fully explain his condition to others, so we do it for him in a way that a nonagoraphobic can understand and appreciate. Our purpose is to take the mystery out of the condition for both the victim and those who are closely associated with him. Just as you, the sufferer, are unaware of the effect agoraphobia has on others in your life, others often don't recognize how they may be aiding and abetting your condition without meaning to do so. We can show you just exactly what we mean by telling you how this system evolved for Ann and Earl.

"After my first attack," Ann said, "our family doctor really tried to help me. He kept telling me that nothing was physically wrong with me. He had no way of knowing that he was scaring me more by saying that. I wanted something to be wrong physically so that he could fix it. If the problem wasn't outwardly apparent, then I would have to be forced to look inside; that was my biggest fear.

"Earl tried his best for me. He spent hours and hours telling me that I was wonderful, that everything would be just fine, that this was only a temporary feeling which would pass. He went out of his way to make me less afraid: he took me grocery shopping, staying right by my side down every aisle and discussing every selection with me. If I was too scared to go, even with him, he would go by himself with a smile on his face. He made excuses for me when I couldn't think of any, and rescued me every time I thought I needed rescuing. He thought nothing of leaving his already precarious job in the middle of the workday to come home and make me feel better. Though I knew I was asking an awful lot of him, I couldn't seem to stop myself.

"We carried on like this until summertime, with me

doing too little and Earl doing too much. Finally, I began to feel that something had to change. I picked up the phone and called the psychologist who had been recommended to me many months before by our physician. Naturally, Earl drove me to that first appointment and waited patiently for me to spend my first hour in therapy. By this time, I think, Earl was as sick of how I was acting as I was, and he would have done just about anything to get us back to normal. It turned out that he had to do a bit more than he anticipated. My first hour with my new psychologist, Tom, went pretty well in that he didn't seem as alarmed by my state as I thought he might have been. He calmed me down, and told me that he treated lots of people with anxieties and that as far as he could tell, I hadn't lost my marbles or even shaken them loose. He did, however, insist that Earl be present and take part in any future hours of therapy.

"Earl was none too pleased with this piece of news, but after listening to my frantic pleas for help, he agreed to participate. I think we both thought that Tom believed the trouble was in the marriage, and we both took offense at that. We couldn't see what Tom saw: the marriage *was* in trouble. Our whole relationship was changing in response to my agoraphobic condition, but it was happening so gradually that neither of us could see how differently we were behaving toward each other. When we fell in love, each of us had been attracted by the independence of the other. We had delighted in the fact that we each had strong convictions and opinions about how to enjoy life, raise children and get the jobs done. My intense anxieties forced both of us into unfamiliar roles. As each new set of fears and avoidances crept up on me, Earl had to take on more and more of my responsibilities. His willingness to shoulder any task that seemed too hard for me to handle assured me that ours was a perfect love, so I gladly gave up making even the smallest decision on my own. I wouldn't dare question his judgment on any issue.''

You would have had a hard time convincing Ann, who felt so bad, that she was getting anything good out of agoraphobia. In reality, though, she no longer had to perform any task or enter any situation that made her feel the slightest discomfort. Earl was the one waiting in line at the department store, jockeying for position in the crowded grocery, waiting in the dentist's office while one of the children had his teeth cleaned. Was he gaining anything? Sure! He was in the driver's seat (figuratively and literally) and was being worshiped for it.

Both Ann and Earl were the beneficiaries of secondary gains—a term used by the helping profession to describe the "goody" you get out of a rotten situation. These gains may not be apparent to those who benefit from them because the focus of concern is placed on the bad circumstances. Secondary gains can be a major problem in overcoming agoraphobia. The agoraphobic who looks to others to perform or help perform his chores never has to take full responsibility for his actions. The limitations produced by agoraphobia can also create opportunities for others to gain. Sally, aged twenty-four, and her husband had been married for four years and were the parents of a baby girl. Her husband's work required him to be away from home a good deal of the time, but when he *was* home, he made life miserable for Sally. He made no effort to understand what she was feeling, and refused to acknowledge that she had a problem. He believed that all Sally had to do to straighten out her life was quit bellyaching and get moving. He treated her like his child, never allowing her to feel that she could or should be responsible for anything. He carefully doled out the household money to her and then expected a full accounting of her expenditures, always ready to criticize her for purchases he deemed unnecessary. At the same time, he constantly castigated her for being such a baby.

Sally's mom brought her to group each week, and Sally had to hide from her husband the fact that she had earned the money for her therapy by altering clothes. She was certainly in a "no-win" situation, and she desperately wanted to find a solution. Driving was one of her avoidances, and in order to get into the car to practice, she had to face his wrath. (He honestly wanted her home all the time.) It's pretty easy to see Sally's husband's secondary gains: he had complete control and power over his wife. Sally's secondary gains may not seem too apparent, but they are there nonetheless. Sally was not just avoiding driving, Sally was avoiding taking charge of her life. As long as she allowed this system to operate, she didn't have to face growing up. Both Sally's secondary gains and her husband's impeded her recovery.

On the other hand, consider Nat, sixty-five, who is retired and living alone. Nat's fear was that he believed he was having a heart attack every time he panicked. He probably spent more time in doctors' offices in one year than most of us spend in a lifetime. Every single time he went to the doctor, he was assured that his heart was just fine and that there was nothing to worry about. Agoraphobia was a lousy companion for Nat, but it did force him to make contact with people he thought might care about him—his doctors and, later on, us. When he began working on his program for recovery from agoraphobia, he really had to work at self-motivation. He was neither as "hindered" as Sally nor as "helped" as Ann, and because of his age, he was only too happy to risk some new feelings if it meant the end of his fears. Because Nat had so *few* secondary gains involved in his condition, he made a productive and speedy recovery.

It is important to think about what we have to *lose* when we let go of agoraphobia. Ann had to reclaim responsibility for her life. Sally had to take a look at her marriage and face the hard work involved in changing the system on which her marriage had been based. Looking carefully at our own motives is an experience we often avoid; but the honesty and commitment that spring from this long and arduous scrutiny are wonderful first steps toward real maturity.

Because agoraphobia involves others as well as ourselves, there are ways our families and friends can help us establish a productive atmosphere for learning and changing. It is your job to set the guidelines for this support. Understand your condition so well that you can discuss it objectively. You will be surprised at how much of your own fear you can dispel as you describe agoraphobia to another person. You will also be hearing yourself give a positive prognosis for recovery.

Ann was scared to death to tell her children about her

condition, so for the years she was struggling with the problem, and also during her recovery, she kept it from them. When she finally "spilled the beans," they received her news as though she had confessed to having had a mild case of the measles. The people we associate with aren't as afraid of agoraphobia as we are, and they don't view us as crazy, sick or nonfunctioning the way we view ourselves. So go ahead and feel O.K. about describing and explaining this condition.

It is *your* responsibility to be honest in appraising your *own* anxiety, and it is *never* appropriate for someone else to assist you in that appraisal. You know all too well when you are uncomfortable and when it would be more productive to leave than to stay; your companion should be only understanding and nonjudgmental. A friend of ours gave us a perfect illustration: he and his wife were very actively working on his new behavior skills, and they were both sure that they were doing a good job. One night, they decided to go to the movies. It had been quite a long time since they had had an outing of this kind, so both partners left home with lots of anticipatory anxiety. As they waited in the ticket line, John was feeling really proud that he was allowing himself to feel comfortable. All of a sudden, his wife turned to him with a concerned expression and said, "How are you doing, darling? Are you feeling O.K.?" John took this as a cue to immediately think that maybe he shouldn't be feeling so good and that if his wife was nervous and worried about his waiting in line, then he should be too.

Sometimes it is difficult for those around you to know just how much time and effort it takes for you to learn new living skills. In fact, you may have to *make* time to practice your new thoughts and behaviors. It is imperative that others be willing to do some of your chores and to do *without* some of your attention. To keep resentment down and morale high, you need to fully explain your needs and your goals. It may be hard for you to remember that asking others to help you is neither unnecessary nor selfish. Your personality makes you feel that you should be able to "handle" this job of recovery without enlisting help. The truth is, you are being selfish when you consistently rob others of the chance to feel good about lending a hand.

Everyone around you reacts one way when you are in the agoraphobic system and quite another when you put it behind you. Faison and Millard were married during the time that Faison was suffering with agoraphobia; from the very beginning of their life together, it affected their interaction. Just as Faison's behavior was altered by the condition, so was Millard's. Millard would be ready and available to rescue Faison if it was convenient for him. However, there was never a question of Faison's dependency on Millard. As Faison began to grow out of her fears, Millard was forced into changing his actions and reactions toward his wife. Almost without his being aware of it, he had lost the girl who counted on him so fiercely and found himself married to a very independent and purposeful woman. Faison's recovery from her thirteen-year condition almost blew her marriage to pieces. She says: "My relationship with the world changed, and so did my marriage relationship. After my recovery from agoraphobia, I stood up for myself. I became assertive, and calmly so. Millard couldn't believe that I was his old Faison acting in this way. It really worried him. He didn't know what I would do next, and he was no longer fully in control of me. Perhaps I was a bit too pushy—but remember, I had an awful lot to catch up on.'' Millard's and Faison's entire system of living together changed, and new and different compromises had to take place in order for them to establish a more mature and more equitable loving relationship.

The practice of psychotherapy is little different from teaching a classroom of fairly eager third-graders. It is the responsibility of the teacher to offer an explanation of the task and to instruct the class in the appropriate skills. At some point, an important shift is made from teacher to pupil. Those third-graders who do well on a math quiz do so because they have been willing to practice their new skills long enough to make them their own. In the beginning, the pupil may have felt that the teacher alone knew how to divide 737 by 42, but with the shifting of responsibilities, he soon realizes that he too is capable of the task and owns all the necessary skills for accomplishment. Take a moment to remember the pride you felt when you were called to the blackboard and discovered that the problem before you was understandable and solvable.

A good place to witness the way responsibilities shift from one person to the next is within the family system. Newlyweds struggle through the division of income and household responsibilities for many months before settling into roles that work best for them. As children come along, parenting responsibilities are added to the marriage, often producing a period of unrest between husband and wife as tasks are once again divided and negotiated. Responsibility roles begin shifting again as each child is taught the importance of being answerable for his actions. Ann says: "The day we taught Albert about looking both ways before crossing the street was a day I felt that shift of responsibility like a ton of bricks. I was frightened for both of us, and terribly proud of him. He was growing up and taking the necessary steps toward being responsible for himself. Today he is driving his own car, and more responsibility has been shifted from me to him. We are both gradually learning to handle our new roles. You will feel the roles of responsibility shift as you begin to participate in your recovery from severe anxiety."

One device that works well for our program participants' family members is a wallet-sized card that Dr. Robin King of CHAANGE developed. This little card suggests seven ways to be helpful to an agoraphobic during the recovery process:

1. Commit yourself to learning about this condition and to providing adult support. Let go of old patterns of overprotecting or demanding and forcing your family member.
2. Have respect for her feelings and yours. Open an honest "airway" of communication between you.
3. Accept his panicky feelings as real and not "weak," imaginary or hysterical. Take care not to belittle, shame or lecture, as this never helps. Remember, his emotional discomfort is legitimate.
4. Acknowledge the first, small changes as her victo-

ries. View continued limitations as temporary—as goals to be achieved as her recovery proceeds.

5. *N*ever attempt to control or "manage" his treatment. Let it be his program. Have him teach you what would be helpful. Let go of parenting him.

6. *G*row with her. Explore new patterns in your relationship based upon mutual respect, not fear and dependency. Accept that even positive changes can require readjustments for all involved.

7. *E*xpect that recovery will unfold as a "process," often two steps forward and one step back. New habits must be learned and reinforced by positive experiences that build confidence.

Read over these suggestions for yourself and then share them with the person or persons most concerned and involved with your condition. The best way to get the help you want is to ask specifically for what you need. As you change your relationship requirements, you may find that you are no longer interested in being involved with people who view life as a set of negative circumstances. Letting go of nonproductive relationships and surrounding yourself with people who tend to bring out the best in you will be part of your growth process. The fact that you have suffered with agoraphobia and are now willing to take steps to confront and undo the fear-enhancing behaviors established because of it will produce a happy bonus for you: you will be building healthy relationships with your family, your friends and your co-workers.

*   *   *

This chapter has concentrated on the important role that others play in your agoraphobic condition and in your recovery. Spend some time thinking about:

1) The fact that others are indeed affected by what you are feeling and how you are reacting to those feelings.
2) Secondary gains. As hard as it is to realize, you are probably gaining something from your condition, and it will help you to recognize what that something is.
3) How others may also be receiving a few secondary gains from your condition and how their reluctance to give them up can hinder your progress.
4) Ways in which you can enlist some positive help and support from your family and friends as you work on your recovery process.
5) The fact that others will change their reactions to you as you develop positive, fear-free behaviors.

Chapter

8

▼▼▼▼▼▼▼

Sexual Distress

▲▲▲▲▲▲▲▲

SEXUAL DIFFICULTIES and distress are not unique to the agoraphobic. Most adults experience some sexual distress at various periods in their lives; it is part of the human condition. Often, the agoraphobic spends so much energy on anxiety that there is little left to nurture the sexual response. The good news is that your sexuality is intact, but may need a bit of nudging from you. The rest of the good news is that allowing yourself to comfort and be comforted sexually, to feel and to experience your sensuality, will help move you *out* of anxiety and not, as you may have thought, deeper into its grip.

When a person is suffering with agoraphobia and is constantly monitoring each and every thought, worrying about what is normal or abnormal becomes almost an obsession. As agoraphobics, we find it hard to believe that there is anything normal about our reactions to panic, and we naturally question all our other actions and reactions. We analyze constantly, trying to decide if our thoughts have become bizarre or abnormal. We compare ourselves unfavorably with others—people we know, as well as people we read about. Magazine articles about the "whens" and "hows" of satisfying sex seem to point up our vulnerabilities and shortcomings, investing them with an authority they do not warrant. Desperately seeking to be a part of the "norm" creates more anxiety for us because we have to fight back the natural urge to allow our singularly individual personality and character to peep through.

In today's supposedly open society, books and articles are cranked out by the score; each seems to offer yet another approach to satisfying sex. If we were to believe everything we read or see on TV, we could assume that sex is the number one preoccupation of all living creatures on this earth. In reality, getting through the day—working, playing, caring for ourselves and others—is our main concern. Intimate, satisfying sexual contact can be a happy bonus.

Sex *can* be a terrific anxiety reducer; however, if you are feeling anxious, you won't feel particularly open to sexual advances. Anxiety produces the need to hold all emotions in check and to fend off any outside stimulation. Your desire to protect yourself from further onslaughts of fear and panic is totally understandable; but being overly protective only leads to more worry, which short-circuits any chance for some welcome relief. Sexual worries and distress are common to the agoraphobic condition, and those which you are experiencing are most probably no different from the ones we have experienced or that have been reported to us by our agoraphobic clients.

Some of the sexual worries that have been expressed are: (a) a fear that sexual intercourse can bring on severe panic or heart attack; (b) worries about performance—a man may worry that his anxiety will prevent erection from taking place, a woman may worry that orgasm will be impossible; (c) fears of losing total control of sanity, of self and of emotions should orgasm in fact occur; (d) concern about too much desire, or too little; (e) doubts and fears about the partner's willingness to understand your apprehensions and remain loyal in spite of them; (f) obsession with thoughts that appear sexually aberrant and frightening in nature.

Obsession with frightening thoughts is a theme spoken over and over again by persons who fear their control is slipping away. In our efforts to clarify this thought pattern to other agoraphobics, we use the phrase "weird thoughts" because it is so descriptive of what is taking place. An example of a "weird thought" is that of the woman who has worried obsessively that she might be homosexual, despite the facts that (a) she has never had a homosexual contact and (b) she is involved in a long-term, mutually satisfying heterosexual relationship. She can still search for, and find, "evidence" that frightens her about her sexual orientation and what that might mean. Another common example is that of the man whose "weird thought" is that he might suddenly be compelled somehow to fondle a strange woman on the subway. He can't imagine where this thought came from and what its implication is, so he worries often and actively. "Weird thoughts" are usually aggressive or sexual in nature and appear to be totally out-of-character to the person who has them. Agoraphobics feel quite sure that *normal* people don't have these kinds of thoughts and that to reveal them would guarantee their place in an insane asylum. The reason that these thoughts tend to involve aggressively hostile acts or sexual behaviors is that most of us grew up believing that these kinds of feelings either were wrong or, at the very least, should be tucked well out of the sight of others. For example, the first time Ann heard the word "masturbation" was at age sixteen, and she was somewhat repelled because she had long since developed the notion that touching her own body was definitely *not* what "good girls" did.

Parents have the awesome responsibility of teaching their children acceptable behavior. Society dictates what that acceptable behavior is; and in our society, it is certainly not acceptable behavior to end a quarrel by bashing your sibling over the head with a book. To nip unacceptable behavior in the bud, a parent will halt the action and, more often than not, leave the child's feelings unaddressed. The truth is that we all feel hostile from time to time, and it is O.K. to have our hostile feelings. We are also sexually aroused by all kinds of stimuli. The trouble crops up only when severe anxiety and panic cause us to think that we can no longer trust ourselves to act in an acceptable manner. In truth, there is no reason to believe that you will act on a fantasy without a conscious decision to do so. Even if you picture yourself hurting someone, it doesn't mean that you *want* to do it or that you *will* do it. You are capable of it, and so are we, but we don't act on that capability.

The same is true for a sexual "weird thought." Consider our previous example of homosexual worries. You have always been heterosexual and suddenly find yourself having homosexual fantasies. The mere fact that you have had panicky feelings which now seem uncontrollable to you does *not* mean that you have lost your ability to judge for yourself what is acceptable for you and what is not. In many ways, you are more controlled during anxiety than you need to be, and are only too watchful of every action and deed.

Sexually arousing books and magazines are everywhere, and the common thread among them is "the kinkier the better." We cannot escape the fact that there are hostile people in this world who perform unthinkable acts of aggression and terror. During any given day, normal, healthy human beings *think* these kinds of thoughts and then dismiss them because they have no relevance to the lives they choose to lead. On the other hand, when we are feeling anxious and unsure of ourselves, we allow these thoughts to linger, trying desperately to analyze not only the thoughts but also our obsession with them. What you must try to understand is that none of us is judged by his thoughts. A tiny bit of philosophy here would be: "Think anything you want, feel any feeling; act on what you choose to." If a particular thought is bothering you, know that you can throw it out, and that it is not necessary to analyze *why* you thought it in the first place. Ann says she used to believe that if people could read her mind, they would know just how crazy she was. We have both long since learned not only that no one can read our minds, but that our thoughts are no weirder than anybody else's. Yours aren't either!

Agoraphobics often complain of a lack of desire for sexual contact. Sexual desire is not going to magically reappear without some effort on your part. We understand that you are vulnerable and self-protective; but your sex life represents an opportunity for you to take an active role in anxiety reduction. Nothing is more comforting to a frightened person than being held by someone who is loved and trusted. Don't deny yourself this comfort. Your desire can be rekindled with the help of an understanding partner. If intercourse seems too invasive or frightening, begin the reawakening process by allowing yourself to be held and to hold. Desire springs from our need to be caressed and comforted; the actual sex act is merely the period at the end of the sentence. Therapists often advise couples who are having sexual difficulty to refrain from intercourse for a specified length of time. During that time, the couple is encouraged to reacquaint themselves with hugging, kissing, petting and soothing; by removing the pressure of an ultimate conclusion, you can progress as slowly as you choose and perhaps be pleasantly surprised by feelings you have been suppressing.

* * *

We hope you have learned that:

1) Sexual difficulties are not unique to agoraphobics.
2) "Weird thoughts" of both aggressive and sexual natures are commonplace and need not be feared.
3) *You* can make a difference in your own sexual responsiveness.

Chapter

9

Defenses

DEFENSE MECHANISMS are the armor we use to protect our emotional and physical selves. We each have our own unique system of defenses to protect the vulnerable inner self. This armor enables us to function in the face of difficult and threatening situations. However, it can also become a rigid shell that incapacitates us from taking action. It is tough and sometimes painful to identify your defenses, but it's necessary: the more we know about ourselves and the way we work emotionally, the more active are our choices in dealing with our inner emotional lives. Insight and freedom do not always go hand in hand, but insight can lead to your being able to practice new behaviors so that freedom results.

The most obvious pattern of protection for the agoraphobic man or woman is that of *avoiding* places, people and things that may trigger anxious responses. To some extent, we all do this and have done it for most of our lives. Millard avoids going with Faison when she shops for clothes; it makes him nervous and embarrassed to wait outside a ladies' dressing room. *His avoiding is a defense.*

The avoidance behavior developed by agoraphobics is one component in a whole system of defenses, and is the part that is most difficult to conceal from others. You can't drive; you can't stay home alone; you can't go shopping. Though these avoidances may be your defense against anxiety, they often produce *additional* anxiety when you are unable to explain your need for them.

There are many defense mechanisms that are not as obvious as avoidance. Procrastination is used as a defense against possible failure. A consistently cheerful facade can be a defense against overt criticism. Sarcasm is a defense against insecurity. Childishness is a defense against taking responsibility for oneself.

Another component of the defense system developed by an agoraphobic may be the habit of concealing emotions, if that person has been taught that an overt show of emotion is improper and shameful. This habit may become so firmly established that the agoraphobic has great difficulty knowing *what* he feels!

Defenses begin innocently as experimental behavior. Our relationships with family, teachers and schoolmates helped shape our defenses. Many of us maintain protective mechanisms that we would do well to examine closely to see if they still serve a purpose. It is possible that what made Andy like you in first grade is no longer useful, now that you're grown and haven't seen Andy in twenty-five years.

We have prepared a list of several typical protective

mechanisms, drawing upon our own personal experiences. Do any of these describe the way you habitually relate to others? Do you recognize any unnecessary defenses? Is it possible that some of your defenses are *adding* to the tension and stress that is already present in your life? Don't be surprised or alarmed to find yourself in any or all of these descriptions.

PROTECTIVE MECHANISMS

WORRY

DESCRIPTION:	You devote perhaps several hours each day to your worry habit, believing that this attention will forestall disaster.
CONSEQUENCE:	You are unhappy, anxious and not a whole lot of fun to be around. Others become exasperated with your need for constant reassurance. This mechanism causes your dialogue to be future-oriented and negative.
SUGGESTION:	Understand that worry has no power to affect the future in any positive way. If you have a concern that needs your thoughtful attention, consciously limit the amount of worry time you will devote to that concern.

SARCASM

DESCRIPTION:	You don't feel secure in making honest declarations of your feelings, needs and desires. As a result, the statements that you make are almost always in opposition to your intent.

CONSEQUENCE: People are on guard around you and wonder whether to trust you. They are likely to be defensive and sarcastic in return; you don't get what you want, and your feelings are hurt. Being sarcastic is exhausting.

SUGGESTION: Substitute straight talk for the sideways method of communication that sarcasm is. Practice until you feel comfortable asking for what you want and saying what you *really* mean.

CATASTROPHIZING

DESCRIPTION: You fear dire consequences, and feel compelled to expect the worst. You attempt to defend yourself against the possibility of disastrous surprise by imagining the worst possible scenario, always clinging to the hope that the actuality will fall short of your expectations.

CONSEQUENCE: You are unable to enjoy the moment, fearing that disaster lurks just around the corner. You are tense, nervous, worried and may have difficulty sleeping.

SUGGESTION: It is always a better choice to make a *realistic* assessment of the situation, deciding for yourself how much control you have over what will happen and how much of that control you wish to exercise. Remember, there is *always* an argument to challenge the likelihood of a catastrophe.

Practice looking for the positive alternative. Catastrophizing is nothing more than an exercise of the imagination.

JUDGING

DESCRIPTION: Fearing rejection, you mask your low self-esteem by being openly critical of others. Like Woody Allen, you wouldn't want to belong to any club that would have *you* as a member! You have gotten to the point that you rarely see good in anyone around you and are quick to jump to negative conclusions about everybody. People let you down and displease you. You're very hard on your family and friends.

CONSEQUENCE: You give the impression that you really don't like or need people very much, when just the opposite is true. This mechanism of judging (rejecting) others often backfires, leaving you hurt and alone.

SUGGESTION: Allow *yourself* the luxury of being imperfect and capable of making mistakes. Our imperfections are what make us interesting, special, vulnerable and, most of all, lovable. Practice focusing on what you *like* and admire about an individual; give compliments. Listen for compliments that may come your way and learn to accept them graciously, without feeling that you have to discount them.

HELPLESSNESS

DESCRIPTION: You have learned to behave in a helpless manner in order to defend yourself against having to make decisions or take responsibility.

CONSEQUENCE: This is a two-edged sword. You may experience temporary relief from anxiety by allowing others to care for you and take charge of your life. However, you run the risk of becoming *so* dependent that you lose your ability to trust your own judgment. Self-doubt increases your anxiety.

SUGGESTION: Set some *realistic* goals for yourself and begin working toward them, without revealing them to anyone. Enjoy each small successful step along the way and then delight in the revelation of your achievement!

REPRESSION

DESCRIPTION: You expend a lot of energy displaying a calm exterior. Your purpose in this is to defend yourself from exhibiting the anxiety you feel. In order to do this, you must repress healthy and powerful emotions.

CONSEQUENCE: When you repress emotions in order to protect yourself from feeling life's pain, you rob yourself of life's pleasures. You begin to feel insubstantial and may have difficulty making appropriate responses.

SUGGESTION: Laugh as hard as you want; cry as much as

you want. Know that you can stop anytime you want. Don't be afraid to let others see and respond to your humanness, realizing that this very quality is part of what draws people to one another.

DENIAL

DESCRIPTION: You refuse to recognize the implications of certain emotional problems by denying their existence. You think that if you ignore the problem you can somehow defend yourself from having to own up to it.

CONSEQUENCE: Problems grow and fester, despite your refusal to acknowledge them. You may have gotten so "good" at denial that it has become difficult for others to communicate with you.

SUGGESTION: Be open to the suggestions of others. Be willing to reveal your concerns to an objective listener. More often than not, that person will be able to dispel most of your fears by helping you put them into perspective. Asking for help is a show of *strength*, not weakness!

BLAMING AND RATIONALIZING

DESCRIPTION: Nothing is ever really your fault. The world is against you. You did the best you could, but circumstances prevented you from reaching your goals. Blaming everybody but yourself for your own state of affairs is your way of defending your inability to take charge.

CONSEQUENCE: You alienate others with your blaming behavior and they may even be frightened of you. You feel paralyzed and incapable of doing anything that will have a positive impact for you. Because circumstances seem to be controlling you, your motivation is not to take charge, only to blame.

SUGGESTION: You need to accept your own imperfection. This will lessen the pressure and bitterness you feel at not living up to your expectations. You will probably begin to notice that people are responding to you more freely, and you will feel less anxious. Once you claim your own mistakes and limitations, you can then take full credit for your successes and your attributes. You will be pleased to discover that your assets outweigh your limitations, by far!

SUBLIMATION AND RUNNING AWAY

DESCRIPTION: You devote all your nonwork hours to hobbies and home improvements. You are always "busy" and have no time for intimate relationships and introspection. You are afraid to look at your own problems, defending yourself against the possibility of having to confront a less-than-perfect self.

CONSEQUENCE: People think you are unfeeling. Although

your accomplishments may be many, your aversion to intimacy in relationships makes it difficult for anyone to "get through" to you. You are more comfortable when you are busy because your anxiety increases when you are forced to slow down.

SUGGESTION: Changing this habit does not mean giving up outside activities that bring you pleasure. It *does* mean making time for the "care and feeding" of your personal relationships. It *does* mean recognizing the need to attend to your emotions and feelings. Awareness is step one.

Looking back at our own experiences, we can show you how our protective mechanisms worked. Faison remembers:

"With my first psychiatrist, I *denied* that I needed his services. I never questioned the medication he prescribed or his reason for doing so; I never actively participated in my treatment. I *blamed* him because he couldn't 'fix' my hurting immediately, and finally dropped out of therapy with no more understanding of what I was experiencing than I'd had when I went to see him the first time.

"The second psychiatrist was a handsome, dashing fellow. I alternately *catastrophized* my situation and *denied* that anything at all was wrong with me. I tried to be cute with him and talked about social things and cars (he drove a Jaguar sedan that I very much admired), anything at all to keep from revealing who I was and what I was feeling. The result was that I didn't get any help from him either, and so began *blaming and rationalizing* again.

"Right about the time I was to see psychiatrist number three, I had an appointment with a medical doctor who was new in town. I very selectively described my symptoms to him, choosing only those I thought he could treat. Finally, he decided that an inner-ear infection was causing my dizziness and nervousness. I was thrilled with his opinion but, at the same time, doubtful that I could have had an undetected ear infection for two years. Timidly, I broached this thought to him, but he assured me that I could have a chronic, recurring infection and that it could be responsible for the feelings I had described. How thrilling it was to pretend for a day or two that he was right—when all along I knew he wasn't. I had withheld *(denied)* information from him just because I wanted so much for him to find a physical cause for my symptoms.

"*Worry* was ever-present during those early years of agoraphobia, when I was still chasing a physical diagnosis for my problems. On two different occasions, I persuaded a physician to arrange for neurological tests (complete with EEG). It was an expensive and time-consuming ordeal, and didn't really need to be done. I felt the need to put myself through these tests to *rationalize* to myself that I was doing all I could to help myself. I was highly critical *(judgmental)* of the doctors for not having suggested these tests themselves."

RESISTANCE

Conceptually, much of the material in this chapter has implied the need for you to give up or let go of agoraphobia and agoraphobia-related thinking and behavior. *Letting go is the essence of recovery.* Letting go is difficult because you need (1) information and (2) new behavior skills. Both of these can be supplied (or taught) you by someone else. But there is something further that you must understand in order to let go. That something is the universal, human tendency to *resist*.

It is a shame that resistance has had such bad press, because it does have a positive side. Resistance keeps us from being easily brainwashed and bamboozled and gives us individual integrity of personality. Our resistance to being molded and pushed and prodded by others begins early; it is made famous by "terrible two-year-olds" the world over. The stronger we are, the more strongly we are able to resist. If we waste any time and energy feeling bad about ourselves for resisting, *that* is resisting. It is part of who we are, and it is as fruitless to hate that in ourselves as it is to hate that our hearts beat involuntarily. We do it because we're human; we're human because we do it.

If resistance is so inherently human and beyond our control, why are we talking about it? Because there are times when it is both useful and appropriate to examine our resistance to see whether it is helping us or hindering us. When we find that we aren't making sufficient headway, in spite of the fact that we have at our disposal all the tools and skills for making changes, we need to examine the possibility that we may be resisting our own recovery! This can certainly be the case for chronic agoraphobics. It was for Faison, who says:

"No one ever wanted to get over agoraphobia more than I did. I hated having lost every minute of those thirteen years, and I grieved over that. I have often said that I missed my twenties, and in a real sense, I did. I certainly didn't have the freedom that most of my contemporaries had. I hated the fact that I had to spend so much money on doctors and tests. I hated having to sit in a psychiatrist's waiting room, worried that someone I knew might walk in at any time. I hated having to lie to my family and friends about why I couldn't go to church, to restaurants, to movies. I hated the humiliation, the despair and the belief that I would spend the rest of my days feeling too nervous to really live.

"To me, that sounds like the description of a person who would be eager to change; a person who would do anything reasonable in order to move out of the condition of agoraphobia. But I was frightened at the thought of changing my behaviors, no matter how negatively they were affecting me. I was not convinced that anything I was being told to do would work, and I was skeptical of those who made suggestions to me. I always felt that I was different from all the others, that my condition was somehow much worse than any case heretofore seen in the annals of agoraphobic treatment. I practiced resistance daily until I decided to give it up."

Some of the examples of resistance we have heard are:

- "I can't get over this. I have had it all my life."
- "I have been to three clinics and nine psychiatrists and no one has been able to help me. See how I've tried? *They* just didn't help me."
- "My husband does not understand. He makes fun of me and threatens to leave me. This is keeping me from being able to practice in a stress-free environment. I just know that I will never get well."
- "I have tried every drug there is. I just can't work on this until the anxiety goes away."
- "Mine is different. I can go anywhere I want to; I just can't stay home. That is the worst place for me."
- "I have a symptom I have never heard mentioned by any book or therapist. Even though no doctor has ever found anything wrong with me, and seven doctors have said it is anxiety, I know I'll never get over this because I have disoriented feelings"—or blurred vision, or tingling scalp, or confusion, or panic in the night, or panic in the morning, ad infinitum.

ACCEPTANCE

We travel throughout the country speaking to groups, working with our regional CHAANGE therapists and talking openly about our experiences. We do this because we want others to know that there is hope. We have noticed that no matter where we speak, people have invariably heard of Dr. Claire Weekes and have read her wonderful books on the subject of anxiety. One of the things she counsels people to do is "accept the anxiety; do not fight." She encourages us to recognize our capacity to stop resisting through choice. Faison found herself reciting her words day and night (aloud and under her breath) and reading them from a page taped to her bathroom mirror. Accepting feeling anxious is difficult, but resisting change doesn't get you anywhere. What do you have to lose? Nothing but your chronic anxiety.

The concept of acceptance can be a difficult one for people to grasp. How do you accept your anxiety and work to change the way you handle it, both at the same time? Accepting it is *part* of working to change it. That, in itself, is a significant change for you. Acceptance shortens the time it will take for your anxiety to run its course and then dissipate. Remember that the physical part of the anxiety reaction is triggered by adrenaline along a predictable curve. If the physical symptoms are accepted for what they are, and are not feared, they will quickly diminish and your body will again be at rest. When you are unaccepting and fearful, more adrenaline is emitted into your bloodstream, and the reactions are intensified and prolonged.

We have heard people say, "I tried it and it didn't work." A gentleman called us one night when we were on *The Larry King Show* (from Washington, D.C., on Mutual Broadcasting). We had been talking about the value of relaxation. The caller wanted us to know that he had certainly tried relaxation and that without a doubt, it hadn't worked for him. We asked him how often he had tried it. Well, he said, he had tried it once. Once! We paled at the notion that one try could change any established behavior pattern. You must be committed to doing what you need to do for however long it takes until the old habit lets go. It will let go, it must let go, because you are in charge of yourself (and that includes your resistance).

SECONDARY GAINS

We talked briefly in Chapter 7 about secondary gains, and it is useful for us to reexamine the subject as we attempt to understand how they can make it easier for us to resist change. Both of us can see that there were secondary gains for us when we were agoraphobics; many people find this to be true for them as well. However, it is unusual for secondary gains to be so beneficial that the person feels *no* motivation to change. Again, it is important that you examine this question for yourself, thinking of all possible positive consequences of being the way you are. Write them down. Get them out in the open. You *do* have a choice about continuing this way, even though you may be distressed to realize that some good has come from the condition.

What follows is a partial list of secondary gains. The list could be longer and you will no doubt think of examples that we have not included. Remember not to frighten yourself or worry if you should discover that something positive, beneficial or helpful has actually resulted from a bad situation. You can get over agoraphobia and still find ways to get what you want in life!

As you read through this list, think of the first statement as the "bad news" and the statement in parentheses as the "good news," the secondary gain.

"People are really worried about me because of my condition." (It feels good to have so much attention.)

"I can't get into shape because exercise makes me panicky." (I can sit on my duff and eat all I want.)

"My mother comes over every day and calls several times a day to see if I'm okay." (I can remain her little girl/boy.)

"I had to drop out of college because of agoraphobia." (I can blame most of my shortcomings on my agoraphobia. I haven't really been *able* to do what most other people have, and it is not my fault that I haven't lived up to my potential.)

"My husband can't invite guests for dinner because it makes me too anxious." (I don't have to cook gourmet meals or entertain.)

"I can't drive alone." (Because my wife goes everywhere with me, I always know where she is. We have a very close relationship, much closer than most couples I know. We are everything to each other.)

"I can't leave home." (My house and yard are the cleanest and prettiest on the block, and I am very proud of that.)

"I am on disability because of this condition." (That income is so convenient for me. If I get over this, that income will stop.)

"My mother never asks me to help with the family

reunion at her house, and I'm never asked to help at church." (Those things are a hassle anyway, and if I were to get over this, I would be expected to do all these things.)

"Habit is stronger than reason," wrote George Santayana. We love to use the example of the woman who was setting her table for lunch one day. Her kitchen was long and narrow, and her silverware drawer was at the end away from the dining area. It had been this way for years, but on this particular day, she decided to move the silverware to a more convenient location. She cleaned out a drawer close to the dining room, and carefully arranged the silver inside, relocating its contents to the drawer that had formerly housed the silver. At dinnertime, she went straight to the old location for the silverware, and found herself doing that on and off for weeks. It took time and repetition to establish the habits that have kept you from reaching your full potential, and it will take time, repetition and *determination* to change them.

*　　*　　*

The purpose of this chapter is to introduce you to your defenses, the protective system you've developed over a lifetime. We hope you have learned that:

1) All of us defend our vulnerable selves with habitual styles of reacting. Some may be more positive than others, and we hope you have begun to recognize some of your own, and identified some that you will want to change.

2) Resistance is a protective system. It is neither good nor bad, though there are times when we can resist too heavily and too long. Awareness of our particular resistance patterns gives us the power to choose to alter them and to find the motivation to move on.

3) Acceptance is a concept that is powerful, though often misunderstood in connection with anxiety and agoraphobia. No one wants to accept the fact that he will feel anxious, but acceptance is step one in moving past the anxiety. It is the tool that defuses the power of the anxiety reaction.

4) When people hear about secondary gains, they tend to feel guilty and judged, as though the condition were self-imposed for a purpose. The term "secondary gains" does not imply that; it *does* imply that certain events and certain family systems can make it difficult for the suffering person to have sufficient motivation to endure the pain of changing.

Chapter

Taking Responsibility

▲▲▲▲▲▲▲

AGORAPHOBICS LEARNED the meaning of responsibility at a very early age. Very often, family situations forced us into taking on emotional burdens we were not ready for. As adults, we take on too much, work too hard and beat ourselves up unmercifully when we feel we have left a job undone, or not performed up to our exacting standards. Perhaps this overzealousness comes from our need to take control, or from our fear of rejection, or perhaps it is a combination of both.

One of the reasons we are so devastated by our condition is that we perceive that we are shirking our duties. We received a heartbreaking letter from a new grandmother who wrote to tell us that she wanted to care for her eight-month-old grandson so her daughter could enjoy a much-needed weekend rest, but she was afraid she might have a panic episode that would prevent her from giving the best care possible to the baby. We know that she wouldn't let herself or her grandson down, but *she* didn't know that, and robbed herself of one of life's sweetest experiences.

On the other hand, we're terrific at avoiding responsibility for our condition. Ann worked with a therapist for two years in an attempt to overcome agoraphobia, without making any progress. Why? She says:

"I wanted my therapist to assume the full responsibility for my condition, and to summon up his mystical powers to banish my anxieties. Because he was the doctor and I was the patient, I didn't feel I had to participate, any more than I would participate in an appendectomy."

The only person who can make you feel good about you is you. Anyone who has recovered from agoraphobia will tell you that he knew he was getting better when he was able to say "I am responsible for my own condition, and for my recovery from that condition."

We feel that we have a responsibility to offer you as many productive alternatives to the anxiety reaction as possible; it is your responsibility to choose and use the ones that work best for you.

SUPPORT

It is natural to want to cling to a helping hand when confronted with pain or adversity. We want it, you want it and there is absolutely nothing abnormal or cowardly about the desire for support.

We have found that when a person begins our program, he believes that he needs three things to see him through: (1) somebody to tell him what to do; (2) somebody to motivate him into doing it and (3) somebody to *do it* with him. These "wants" are no surprise to us, because we certainly felt the very same way. Ann learned early in her agoraphobic condition that she could undertake almost anything as long as her husband was close beside her, and soon learned to feel lost and frightened when he wasn't available. While there are all kinds of therapies available to agoraphobics (and some of them do suggest the assignment of a "support person"), we believe that this causes more anxiety than it eliminates. The agoraphobic tendency is to lean heavily on the supporter and to feel frightened and abandoned when forced into facing situations alone. It seems to us that it is far better to learn to take small steps alone, building self-confidence with each one, than to develop the notion that there is something so wrong that it takes two to do the job of one.

We needed support during our recovery, and you need support during yours. But what you need is the kind of support that connotes faith in your abilities, along with a big dash of tenderness and understanding. That is the kind of support we give to the participants in the CHAANGE program and the kind that you will want to enlist from your family and friends.

PURPOSE

The best way we know to begin taking responsible steps away from anxiety is to apply the concept of purpose, constantly reminding yourself of your reason for doing something or for going somewhere. This will reduce your anxieties immeasurably.

Agoraphobics (and we like to think it is because we are so creative) have trouble sorting things out and taking steps one at a time. Ann says she's never been able to break the habit of taking on too much, planning too many activities or moving too fast, and then becoming overwhelmed by the whole mess. She had avoided driving for so long that the very thought of beginning again could bring about panicky feelings without her even being in close proximity to her car. Somehow, she was convinced she had to overcome *all* her driving fears on that first trip out, and therefore, in her very vivid imagination, one turn around the block appeared as ominous as a road trip from here to eternity! After she got the hang of concentrating on her *purpose* for driving from one place to another, she made much faster progress. She gave up the practice of getting into the car just to see if she would feel anxious; she made sure that she had a good reason for going somewhere, and something productive to do once she arrived. If she felt anxious as she was driving along, she would quickly remind herself that her purpose was to go from point A to point B, not to pass or fail a self-imposed set of requirements.

By sticking to your purpose, not only will you feel less anxious, you will also be taking responsibility for your actions. For example, think about a job you've been putting off for a while and decide now that you are going to tackle it. It doesn't matter whether it's a complicated task (like writing an article on your view of the origin of the species) or a relatively simple task (like weeding last year's herb garden): decide that this is the time to get the job done. Now, think about your very good reasons for performing the task. Perhaps you have always wanted to set Darwin straight on a thing or two; or you know that chives do better in direct sunlight. Once you've got your purpose clear, go to it. Every single time your mind wanders or something interrupts you, remind yourself of your purpose. Soon, you will discover that you are totally absorbed with the task at hand, and you are loving it. It feels good to be making progress at long last, and finally you have discovered what is meant by "the joy is in the doing." Time will fly by. You will even find, to your surprise, that you're a little sad that your task is accomplished.

* * *

Apply the concepts of purpose and responsibility to your anxiety condition. There is absolutely no purpose or reason for staying where you are now. You are obviously reading this book to find ways of feeling better, and we are confident that you are ready to be responsible for your progress. Our hope is that this chapter has helped you recognize that:

1) taking responsibility for your condition and for your recovery is a giant step toward letting go of agoraphobia;
2) you and your strong character are your best support system;
3) finding a purpose, and sticking to it, reduces a lot of unnecessary anxiety.

Chapter

11

▼▼▼▼▼▼▼

How to Begin to Change

▲▲▲▲▲▲▲▲

BEGINNING TO CHANGE is tough, because though most of us are certainly willing to change, we don't want to wait for the natural process to take place. We want it to have happened yesterday. Change occurs systematically, as you will see more clearly in the coming chapter. In *this* chapter we are *preparing* to change—a vital part of that process. Until now, we have been primarily involved in information-giving and you in information-receiving. From this point on, we will be making specific suggestions on what you can *do* to change your behavior.

1. TAKING RISKS

Everyone we've ever met who has a problem with anxiety is wary of changing old thoughts and behaviors. "What if I take this risk and end up in worse condition than before?"

Risk-taking is a positive experience, and one that is essential to the growth process. It *is* hard to take risks, but do you realize the extent to which you do it every day? *Life* is a risk, as much as you may wish it were not. Safety is an illusion—there is no real assurance of external safety. Remember, when you begin to practice new behaviors (change habits), you will be focusing on the *goal* rather than on the risk. The real risk lies in *not* trying to change and, therefore, in never having lived the way you wanted to live.

Have you ever heard of "approach/avoidance conflict"? The words are used to refer to that very human part of our nature which causes us to feel two things at once: both a desire to proceed toward a goal (approach) and, at the same time, a fear of going too close to that goal (avoidance). An example of this is given by Faison: "A neighbor of mine called me hoping that I would adopt a kitten that had strayed into her yard. I stooped in her driveway with a morsel of dry cat food in my hand. The kitten wanted the food but was extremely frightened of leaving its hiding place beneath a low hedge. I coaxed the kitten for the longest time, and it would alternately venture halfway to me and retreat. The encounter ended in defeat for both me and the kitten." Understanding that all creatures experience the "approach/avoidance conflict" gives us the ability to recognize it and to decide to move on past it.

2. DROPPING YOUR "SHOULDS"

This is a good time for you to renounce your perfectionistic "shoulds." We have described them already, and hope that you have given some thought to what your particular "shoulds" may be. "Should," "must," "ought to," "have to," "always," "never"—these are anxiety-producing words that get in your way as you begin working to overcome your condition. Practice letting go of them and changing them now. There *is* no such thing as perfection; relentlessly seeking it only creates anxiety. The way you let go of perfection-seeking is to change your requirements of yourself and others; and a way to start that is to modify what you say to yourself and others. We act as though there were a long list somewhere of things we "should" do and "must" feel. There isn't. So go on—let go of your incredibly difficult (and impossible) expectations. Once you do this, it will be far easier for you to accomplish what you *want to* in your life.

3. EXERCISING YOUR RIGHTS AND RESPONSIBILITIES

You have the right to work toward emotional well-being, toward gaining control of your life. Exercising that right requires that you exercise your responsibility. (You are responsible for doing *all* you are able to do and for *allowing* yourself to try new behaviors and thoughts.) While you are doing this, may we suggest that you engage your sense of humor. Having panic attacks may not seem very funny to you right now, but Ann can always get a laugh with her recollection of the routine she went through before getting into her car: "Thirty minutes before going *anywhere,* I would do my pocketbook checklist. Checkbook (in case I had to write a check for hospitalization or emergency medical services); at *least* three dimes or quarters (one for an emergency call to the doctor, one for an emergency call to my husband, one for an emergency call to my mother, who lived a thousand miles away); a bottle of Pepto-Bismol—*Full* (in case of a sudden attack of stomach miseries); a minimum of fifteen Valium tablets—*Carefully Counted* (for chewing at stoplights); a brown paper bag (blowing into it, I had heard, could counteract hyperventilation); little black book (containing *all* important phone numbers, in case of memory lapse). I didn't care whether the trip was one block or five miles—to be without all this equipment was unthinkable. Carrying this huge pocketbook was a source of comfort, but also anxiety-producing. What if somebody caught a glimpse of the contents? Or *worse*, what if I spilled it? How could I explain? I could just see people imagining me roaring down the highway, *frantically* popping Valium, using Pepto-Bismol as a chaser. Some cocktail!''

You have no doubt heard and read of Norman Cousins, the former editor of *The Saturday Review,* who wrote movingly about his participation in his recovery from lupus in *Anatomy of an Illness.* His recovery, in part, involved laughter. It helped him, it helped us; it can help you too. Cousins never laughed *at* his illness, and we certainly are not suggesting that you do that either. But there is a lot in life which is funny, and we want you to look for it.

4. YOUR CHOICES

Choice is an abstract concept. Viktor Frankl in *Man's Search for Meaning* illustrates this concept with examples from his days in a concentration camp. Everything was taken from him; there were no external choices he could exercise. He could not move without permission, eat without permission, talk without a guard listening nearby. His family was exterminated; all around him people were dying daily. However, he began to realize that he had more power over his situation than the guards did: he had the power to choose how to react to what was going on around him. He could choose whether to become discouraged; whether to give up; whether to love his campmates; whether to harbor his anger. He has based not only that book but his life's practice as a psychiatrist on his discovery of this truth: all persons have choice in all situations.

Faison says: "Dr. Frankl was an inspiration to me. While I was getting over agoraphobia, I was confronted daily with situations that I felt powerless to change. As I began to say to myself 'I have a choice about how I react to this,' I realized that fear was *not* the only choice; there were infinite other choices I could make. I remember one rainy day when the world looked bleak and so did my life. I felt a wave of depression and anxiety sweep over me, and I felt unspeakably sad and alone. For a moment, I wondered if life was worth living. I said to my husband, 'I am so depressed.' He said, 'You don't have to be, you know.' Millard reminded me that I had a choice about how I felt. There is nothing fundamentally depressing about a rainy day. It doesn't have power over you—you do have a choice about how you let circumstances affect the way you feel."

5. BECOMING DECISIVE

Decision-making is a learned behavior, a skill which can be yours. You *can* take charge of your life and make decisions and choices. How do you begin? It is critically important that you set goals for yourself. Goals and objectives help you focus your thoughts and activities. No one can set goals *for* you, so you must sit down with paper and pencil and give some thought to what you wish to accomplish.

Start small. You don't have to do it all the first time. Begin small, building on your successes. Follow through with what you've planned and feel good about that. For Faison, being able to sit through a ten-minute baptismal service was a small goal, but a *big* success. Decisiveness isn't something you attain overnight; it's a skill you build, a little at a time.

6. POSITIVE SELF TALK

Another way to facilitate behavior changes is to listen to the statements you are making to yourself. You will need to change those which are negative and paralyzing. In *Be the Person You Were Meant to Be,** Jerry Greenwald sets forth

---

* New York: Simon and Schuster, 1979. Quoted by permission.

contrasts between attitudes he calls "nourishing" and "toxic." As you begin to change some of your habits, we hope that you will review them frequently. Learning positive self talk helps you change the anxiety habit!

Toxic and Nourishing Living

1. NOURISHING: Do I take the initiative in doing the best I can to get what I need?

    or

    TOXIC: Do I wait and hope that somehow what I need will be brought to me by someone else?

2. NOURISHING: Do I decide what's most important for me?

    or

    TOXIC: Do I allow others to make decisions for me?

3. NOURISHING: Do I give up my attempts to control the world and accept life as it is?

    or

    TOXIC: Do I live my life dominated by fears of catastrophe for which I continuously attempt to prepare?

4. NOURISHING: Am I willing to take reasonable risks and experiment with new behavior that might be more satisfying?

    or

TOXIC: Do I cling to obsolete behavior patterns which mainly offer the security of being familiar?

5. NOURISHING: Do I focus on what I am doing in the here and now?

or

TOXIC: Do I usually wander into fantasies of the future or mistakes about the past?

6. NOURISHING: Do I pay attention to one experience at a time?

or

TOXIC: Do I try to do two things at once and thereby split my attention into pieces?

7. NOURISHING: Do I take for myself the central role of determining my lifestyle?

or

TOXIC: Do I give over this function to others?

8. NOURISHING: Do I take responsibility for satisfying my own needs?

or

TOXIC: Do I try to manipulate other people into doing it for me?

9. NOURISHING: Do I function as best I can in the here and now of my life?

or

TOXIC: Do I cling to the misfortunes and tragedies of

my past (real or imagined) and use these as excuses to avoid taking responsibility for myself in the present?

10. NOURISHING: Do I live my personal life as I see fit and take my chances that some people will reject me?

or

TOXIC: Do I go through life explaining myself and needing everyone's approval?

11. NOURISHING: Do I see life as exciting and stimulating?

or

TOXIC: Do I experience myself struggling to stay alive in a jungle of hostile forces?

12. NOURISHING: Do I see myself as continuing to grow to the last day of my life?

or

TOXIC: Do I create an artificial cutoff (e.g., "After thirty, it's all downhill") and live as if my opportunities for new discoveries and newfound joys were over?

13. NOURISHING: Do I accept my need for other people as part of my lifestyle?

or

TOXIC: Do I "let it all hang out" and if others don't like it, "Who needs them?"

14. NOURISHING: Do I experience my conflicts and "problems" as essentially of my own making?

    or

    TOXIC: Do I project these onto other people and blame them for my troubles?

15. NOURISHING: Is my behavior primarily self-regulating and based on my discoveries of what fits me?

    or

    TOXIC: Do I cling to attitudes instilled in me in my childhood which I am afraid to reject?

16. NOURISHING: Do I accept myself as I am and decide how I wish to change if at all?

    or

    TOXIC: Do I believe that I *must* become a different person in order to live a productive, gratifying life?

17. NOURISHING: Am I willing to take the risks of reaching out for what I want?

    or

    TOXIC: Am I so fearful of rejection that I would rather starve myself emotionally than risk being turned down?

18. NOURISHING: Do I experience my feelings and emotions as valuable parts of myself?

    or

    TOXIC: Do I see them as weaknesses to be controlled and suppressed?

19. NOURISHING: Am I aware of the changing reality of myself and the world around me?

    or

    TOXIC: Do I rigidly insist on my established attitudes and values as fixed and unchangeable?

20. NOURISHING: Do I accept my mistakes as an inevitable part of learning?

    or

    TOXIC: When I do something that displeases me do I attack myself with ridicule, disgust or self-punishment?

21. NOURISHING: Do I focus on the gratifications and meaningfulness of day-to-day experiences as the essence of living a productive life?

    or

    TOXIC: Do I toil without satisfaction, working toward the day when, hopefully, I will "be happy"?

22. NOURISHING: Do I center my attention on appreciating what I enjoy in my experiencing of myself and my world?

    or

    TOXIC: Do I focus on what's lacking or what I find frustrating?

23. NOURISHING: Do I accept myself as I am and continue my growth primarily as something I want for myself?

or

TOXIC: Do I stand condemned in my own eyes as inadequate and seek to "prove" myself by accomplishments or success?

24. NOURISHING: Do I experience my selfishness as an expression of the law of self-preservation?

    or

    TOXIC: Do I believe that "selfishness" is a dirty word?

25. NOURISHING: Do I accept pain as a normal aspect of living and an inevitable aspect of my growth?

    or

    TOXIC: Do I experience pain (anxiety, tension, fearfulness) as something "evil"?

26. NOURISHING: Am I aware that pain is often a valuable message directing my attention toward some frustrated need which I am neglecting?

    or

    TOXIC: Do I consider pain as something to be immediately minimized or eliminated in any way possible?

27. NOURISHING: Is my behavior a reaction to my experiencing of present reality?

    or

    TOXIC: Do I project my past experiences onto the present?

7. NEVER THINK OF FAILING

You can overcome your fear. Some people practice, practice, practice all that we tell them to do. They work on their dialogue and relax their bodies. Even though they do everything in the most cooperative spirit, they really don't expect to succeed; they expect to fail. Dr. Norman Vincent Peale, in his book *You Can if You Think You Can*, advises us to eliminate three words from our vocabulary: Lack, Loss and Limitation.

"I lack confidence."
"I lack 'know-how.' "
"I lack a supportive family."
"I have lost years of my life to this condition."
"I have lost my only chance to be happy."
"I have lost my independence."
"I am limited to staying home."
"I am limited to this unrewarding job because of this
    condition."
"I am limited in my choices."

Drop these words today. Don't brood over past failures. Yesterday is not today. Practice positive thoughts; practice being unafraid; practice being hopeful. And get ready to practice those things you have been avoiding—an exciting journey is about to begin!

*   *   *

Here's what we hope you have learned in this chapter:

1) You have the first tools—understanding and education—to break the agoraphobic cycle.
2) Changing habits involves taking risks. It is to be expected that you will feel some trepidation when you venture into the unknown, no matter how unhappy you are with the state of your life.
3) You have a right and a responsibility to utilize your free choice as a human being. You have a right to work toward good emotional health, and a right to make good decisions for yourself. Set goals for yourself and pursue them enthusiastically.
4) Negative self talk contributes to anxiety. Practice becoming aware of such statements and turning them around to more positive, less anxiety-producing ones.

12

▾▾▾▾▾▾▾

Learning to Swim

▲▲▲▲▲▲▲▲

WE WHO SHARE the personality traits that predisposed us to the anxiety condition want to short-circuit the learning process: we would much rather claim that we already *know* how to do something or *don't know* how to do something, instead of going to the trouble of learning systematically. You may already have a fine intellectual understanding of everything that we're about to tell you, but we don't change our behaviors merely by reading and thinking. We also have to be willing to go through the process of actively changing old behaviors and replacing them with behaviors that will build confidence and eliminate anxieties. The steps necessary for replacing nonproductive habits with productive ones are the steps Ann's son, Albert, took when he learned to swim: understanding, planning, believing and doing.

Ann remembers: "Albert taught himself to swim when he was five years old. That summer, each sunny day would find us trooping down to the lake. Albert would trot behind us, dragging his tiny flotation belt along after him. He would not condescend to wear a life vest when he swam, but felt comfortable and secure with his ski belt as he splashed around in the waters of the lake.

"For weeks, he refused any offers of swimming lessons, and although we were glad that he could be trusted never to jump into the water alone, Earl and I began to wonder if his caution could be indicative of a larger fear. He confused us, though, by his willingness to spend hours on the lake as long as he was safely buckled in his belt. In mid-August, we took a trip to Florida. After a long day of travel, we stopped for the night at a motel with an inviting swimming pool. At the edge of the pool, Albert announced that he could swim quite well, and wouldn't be needing his belt. We protested loudly, insisting that he just didn't realize that the water in the pool was well over his head and that without his belt he would surely sink. Albert would hear none of this, and stubbornly kept assuring us that he knew what he was talking about, and that we should just stand back and watch. Our boy executed a loud dive, touched bottom, pushed off and then performed a magnificent underwater crawl the entire length of the pool! His head would surface every once in a while as he gleefully gulped some air before submerging again. He pulled himself out of the pool with the same assurance as when he entered, surprised that we could possibly have been doubtful. After all, he stated, 'I knew I could do it.' "

How had Albert taught himself to swim? First, he had been motivated to learn by the presence of so many swimmers in his family; all of us shared a love for water. Second, he had spent hours in or around the lake, watching and studying the moves of others, hoping to discover the secret of swimming through observation. Third, Albert began to think like a swimmer; he imagined what it must feel like to float without the support of his belt, relying only on his skills to keep him moving. The countless times that he practiced swimming in his imagination gave him the extra added confidence of truly believing that he *was* a swimmer. His swimming ability may well have been secondary to a greater accomplishment. Albert understood at age five something that had escaped Ann a good part of her life: that there is a *process* of understanding, planning, believing and doing which is absolutely necessary if we are to reach our goals.

Before you begin working on changing avoidance behaviors, it's important to practice changing behaviors that have nothing to do with your anxiety troubles. By going through these exercises, you will be affirming to yourself that you are capable of changing old habits, and you will also be experiencing the effort that it takes to get the job done.

Ann recalls: "My routine was to creep out of bed, go to the bathroom, walk into the kitchen, begin breakfast, drink lots of coffee and smoke cigarettes, clean up the kitchen, then head for the shower. This had been my routine long before I developed agoraphobia, and it didn't seem likely that changing this established pattern could affect how I felt. Every morning, each of us gets out of bed and goes through a routine to which none of us ever gives much thought. My morning activities were so automatic that my mind could be occupied elsewhere. The 'elsewhere' was filled with anticipatory anxiety, so not only was I used to starting my day in my own habitual pattern, I was also used to beginning my morning worried about what perils would befall me during the day.

"Without leaving the security of my home, I began working on little things I could change without frightening myself. I began by setting my alarm clock for thirty minutes earlier than usual. Instead of walking into the kitchen with a cigarette in my hand, I would immediately take my shower, put on my makeup and dress for the day. This took quite a bit of effort, because part of me really wanted to stay in my nightclothes, just in case I should feel the need to go back to bed after the family had left for the day. Getting completely dressed made me feel committed to facing whatever lay ahead, and each day I had to recommit myself to what I felt sure was a better, if not harder, approach. I stopped drinking coffee and forced myself to drink juice and eat something while everyone else was eating. I wouldn't allow myself a moment to sit in anxious contemplation after the last child departed, and began my chores without reading the paper or turning on TV. I built in a little reward system for myself by looking forward to something extra nice for lunch and an hour's nap afterward.

"As I recall for you this first little set of behavior changes, I find myself thinking how simple it all sounds now. It's really hard for me to recall the feeling of effort that it took for me to begin doing something, *anything*, about anxiety. I didn't want to have to do anything differently— I just wanted the bad feelings to go away; I was pleasantly surprised that rearranging some old routines could have a positive impact.''

It is very important that you gain the experience of changing a nonthreatening habit or pattern of behavior so that you can become aware of the effort and commitment this requires. As an experiment, try changing a little habit of yours today. If, for instance, you always put your right leg into your underpants first when you dress, decide that from now on you will start with your left leg. You are going to feel awkward the first few times you dress in this manner, and you may even feel slightly confused. There is also a good chance that you will slip up and dress in your old familiar way and have all of your clothes on before it occurs to you that you forgot to think about which leg was supposed to go into your breeches first. Don't start over; just recommit yourself to thinking about it carefully the very next time you put your pants on. It won't take very long for the new habit to replace the old. After you have proved your ability to change a behavior pattern by working on little things, it will be time to begin working on a new behavior that will help you overcome agoraphobia.

RELAXATION

Learning and utilizing a relaxation technique is the foundation for conquering any anxiety reaction. It is physically impossible to have a panic attack if your mind and body are relaxed. If you don't believe us, try this: Put this book down for a minute and think about a situation that produces anxiety for you. Go ahead and think just how it feels to have an anxiety attack. You will feel your body growing tense just imagining the event and you will begin to feel some of the sensations of panic. As soon as this happens, allow your body to become as limp as a rag doll and slow your breathing by gently resting your hand on your diaphragm so that you can feel the rhythmic rise and fall. Take a moment to realize the difference you are feeling.

Relaxation works so well that almost every health-care facility in this country is teaching its techniques. Childbirth is made much easier using relaxation; high blood pressure can be effectively reduced with these methods; recovering cardiac patients are instructed to use relaxation to reduce stress on their hearts. There is no question that we can greatly lower our anxiety levels by employing this fundamental and easy-to-learn skill. The CHAANGE program begins with a relaxation-exercise cassette and instructions for its use. We ask our participants to practice concentrated relaxation five times a day. It is important to find the exercise that is best for you. Once you have mastered the technique, a one-word cue can bring about an immediate release from stressful feelings. You will be able to use this skill for the rest of your life, not just to deal with your immediate anxiety problems.

Ann uses this exercise: Lie down on a bed, cot or sofa. Make sure that there is nothing pressing against your body, and wriggle around until you have made a comfortable spot for yourself. For the first few minutes, take inventory of each part of your body, assuming the most relaxed position for your feet, legs, buttocks, stomach, hands, arms, shoulders, neck and head. Close your eyes and imagine that you are lying on an inflatable raft just at the shoreline of a beautiful sunny beach. Imagine that you can hear each warm wave as it gently brushes against the bottoms of your feet, and think about how nice the sun feels as it warms your body. You are just where you want to be, without a care in the world, and you are totally at peace.

There is a good friend lying beside you who hasn't been feeling very comfortable for a long time; you have decided to help him learn how to physically relax his body. You quietly ask him to watch and imitate everything you do, and you assure him that he will be totally relaxed when you have finished.

Beginning with your toes, you show your friend how to tighten his toes toward the arch of his foot, holding that position until there is noticeable strain. As you begin to tighten your foot, you instruct your friend to take in a deep breath and hold it until it's time to relax. As you exhale, remind your friend to concentrate on how wonderful it feels to relieve the strain. Working from your feet to your head, you show your friend how to relax each and every inch of his body by first straining the muscle (as he takes a big, deep breath) and then relaxing the muscle (and exhaling).

By the time you have taught your friend how to relax the muscles in the neck and head, both of you are completely relaxed and very still. You quietly enjoy this comfortable state for as long as you like before rising.

Ann feels it has always been easier for her to pretend that she is teaching another person to relax because she is impatient with herself. When she tried to relax, she would get angry if she couldn't do it perfectly. By focusing her attention on an imaginary friend, she could help him over hard spots and give encouragement when necessary. You may well find that you can relax your mind and body by using progressive muscle relaxation without the added imagery. Do whatever works best for you and makes you feel the most comfortable.

SELF TALK

It is important that you change your internal dialogue from nonproductive "self talk" to positive, productive conversation. Thought-switching and positive dialogue are changes in thinking and aren't outwardly apparent. Recovery from agoraphobia requires both cognitive *and* behavioral changes.

The word "cognition" is really a high-sounding synonym for thinking, or information processing. Your cognitions— your daily thoughts about your anxious feelings, about your duties, about what you "should" be doing, how you ought to appear to others—affect your agoraphobia in a way and to an extent that you may never have imagined. Learning that you *can* modify your feelings, thoughts and behaviors, and then doing so, will make the difference between short-term remedy and lifelong cure. Other approaches to agoraphobia treatment tend to leave out this critical step in the learning process and only chip away at the symptoms associated with panic. That is why you may have heard that you can "learn to live" with your limitations. We know that you can learn to live *without* limitations.

Sometimes Ann found that making a behavior change enabled her to develop a more positive dialogue regarding a particular avoidance, and sometimes developing a productive thinking attitude prompted a behavior change. When we are asked to explain the necessity of intertwining these two therapeutic approaches, we like to give the example of a successful dieter. In order for any of us to lose unwanted pounds and maintain our desired weight, we have to change our eating behavior (smaller portions, different cooking methods, high-nutrition/low-fat foods) and change our cognitions ("I feel great every time I meet a challenge head on," "I am so proud of myself for passing up dessert," "Dieting is easier than I expected"). Changing our eating behavior for a short period of time will result in some weight loss, but as we all know, those pounds jump right back on if we don't change the way we think about our eating style. "Thinking" and "doing" creates the best atmosphere for establishing a lifestyle that makes us happy and self-confident. Viewing excess anxiety as ten unnecessary pounds that you are ready to shed might help you realize that your goal is within your grasp. There are specific guidelines to follow for successfully changing your eating habits, and the same is true for habitual avoidance.

TECHNIQUES

The three steps we use for confronting fearful situations are: *ranking, imagery desensitization* and *in vivo desensitization*. Ranking is the arrangement of avoidances according to the amount of anxiety they produce, so that we can begin our work by confronting a situation that produces only a mild amount of discomfort. Imagery desensitization is the process of picturing yourself doing something well, comfortably or fearlessly before you actually do it. In vivo desensitization is the process in which you systematically venture out into the world to confront situations you once avoided. By imagining a successful confrontation with an avoidance, you will greatly reduce the anxiety when you are ready to confront the situation "in vivo" (in actuality).

RANKING

After you have successfully practiced your relaxation skills over a period of days, you will be ready to make a list of avoidances. Number your paper, and beside number 1, describe a situation or event that produces mild anxiety for you. Number 2 will be a situation that produces slightly more anxiety than number 1, and so on down the list until you have ended with the situation that creates the most discomfort for you. Some things on the list may be items you have avoided for many years. Rank them according to the anxiety you feel when you think about the possibility of confronting them. Don't be concerned about the length of your list. Even though you may feel that you are totally aware of what makes you uncomfortable, preparing this list and going through the process of ranking avoidances is in itself a behavior change for you. Your list is your way of defining your fears and bringing them out into the open; you can't solve the problem until you take a look at the equation.

IMAGERY DESENSITIZATION

How many times has the mere thought of a situation made you feel terribly uncomfortable? Imagery desensitization gives us an opportunity to think or imagine a situation the way we would *like* for it to occur. It is a productive planning tool that is not limited to the anxiety condition. Once you have developed this particular skill, you will be able to use it anytime you want to create an atmosphere of success. To practice imagery desensitization, you will need to set aside time for yourself and follow a few specific rules. Assume for a moment that you have decided to work on the first avoidance on your ranking list. Set aside approximately twenty minutes each day for perhaps a week, and go through your planned confrontation in your imagination. Instead of imagining that a catastrophe befalls you, imagine that you will feel comfortable and secure in the situation, filled with confidence about your skills. If, as you are doing this, anxiety creeps into your conscious thoughts, you will stop the imaginary event, use your relaxation technique and then begin again. Depending on the event, it may take days to go all the way through the exercise free of anxiety, but rest assured that you *will* reach the point of being able to think through or imagine a feared situation without having an anxiety reaction.

The twenty minutes a day that you spend with imagery desensitization is enough time to invest in the avoidance behavior that you are working on. This will free you to enjoy yet another new behavior. You have made a decision to work on one behavior at a time, and you are actively working on the chosen behavior each day; therefore, it will not be necessary to fret or worry that nothing is being done about your condition. You can congratulate yourself because you are taking responsibility for your recovery, and spend the rest of your day doing things you enjoy and feeling productive.

IN VIVO DESENSITIZATION

Having someone tell you to "Go ahead and just *do* it" is horrifying for anyone who has ever experienced panic or severe anxiety. Those nasty words lose all of their impact for a well-prepared, take-charge, recovering agoraphobic. You can approach your first in vivo desensitization without fear because you will have spent a good deal of time preparing for a successful venture. The steps you have taken in preparation for this have included: educating yourself about your condition; changing the way you talk to yourself; learning and practicing relaxation techniques; curtailing certain habits (like excessive caffeine intake and poor diet) and practicing imagery desensitization. You will *know* internally and externally that you will be successful because this time, as you attempt to confront an avoidance, you have coping skills that you never had before. The first time Ann drove her car armed with her new behaviors, she erased hundreds of previous failures. It was as if she were experiencing the thrill of driving for the very first time in her life. You will feel the very same way, and we can't help being equally excited for you.

Just giving you a description of these basic techniques isn't enough to get you started on the road to recovery, any more than your having a clear understanding of the problem will make it go away. After you have read over the following examples, take the time to make your own list and plan your work schedule. Here's how Ann's ranking list looked when she began working on avoidance behaviors:

1. *Eating in Restaurants*
   a. standing in line at a carryout
   b. eating in small cafés
   c. going out to dinner with friends
2. *Meetings*
   a. attending with friends
   b. attending alone
   c. making a suggestion or comment
   d. presiding
3. *Shopping Centers*
   a. short trip with husband
   b. short trip with friend
   c. long trip with husband/friend
   d. short trip alone
   e. long trip alone
4. *Elevators*
   a. riding few floors with friend (enclosed elevator)
   b. riding few floors alone (enclosed elevator)
   c. riding many floors with friend (enclosed elevator)
   d. riding many floors alone (enclosed elevator)
   e. riding in glass or exposed elevator with friend
   f. riding in glass or exposed elevator alone

5. *Escalators*
   a. going down
   b. going up
6. *Grocery Stores*
   a. going with husband for few items
   b. going with husband for many items
   c. standing in checkout line with husband
   d. shopping for few items alone
   e. standing in checkout line with half-full basket
   f. shopping alone for many items
   g. standing in checkout line with basket overflowing

[Note that she listed "standing in checkout line" in three places. She meant to!]

7. *Sex*
   a. having none
   b. brief spontaneous encounter
   c. performing with enthusiasm
   d. trying different expressions
8. *Driving Alone*
   a. driving to school (one mile)
   b. driving to grocery store (three miles)
   c. driving into town (ten miles)
   d. driving outside familiar surroundings
   e. driving out of town

You will notice that Ann ranked her avoidances and then went to the trouble of sub-ranking them, or breaking the avoidance behavior down into manageable portions. The sub-ranking is what we call "partializing." It can be overwhelming to try to work on an avoidance by thinking that all the behaviors associated with that avoidance have to be tackled simultaneously. Working on one small section at a time will ensure success and give you the impetus to tackle the whole.

Let Ann tell you how she began working on her driving avoidance:

"I started with 8-a—driving to Bell School, a distance of one mile. My motivation for wanting to drive to Bell School was great: Albert and Catherine were both enrolled in this tiny country school, and I knew every teacher and most of the children by name. I was always greeted warmly and thanked profusely for any help that I was willing to give. The *only* thing preventing me from going to the school to work in the library or help in the lunchroom was my fear of driving down that road.

"One quiet Monday morning, I began my imaginary trips to Bell School, down McFarland Road. I mapped out in vivid pictures my entire trip to and from school. That first day of imagining my trip was pretty tough, because I kept feeling anxious at some point along the way and needed to use my relaxation over and over. Tuesday's 'head trip' was somewhat easier, and by Friday I could really see progress. Once I was able to think about going without anxiety, I began to believe that I could do it. Rather than set up an actual appointment to visit school, I decided to just drop in unannounced on a day when I felt ready. Early the next week, I wanted to try the drive. I was definitely anxious as I started out, but I expected that I would be, considering all the times I had tried in terror to make this trip. Deliberately driving slowly and forcing myself to look at all the houses, yards and farmland that I had imagined so well, I moved forward. I pulled into the Bell School parking lot and literally saluted the building. The exhilarating effect of this little trip lasted for days, and for the first time in years, I could see the end of my struggles with driving.

"My driving experiences didn't always seem as exciting or go as smoothly as that first trip back to Bell School, but I refused to allow the uncomfortable days to have a devastating influence. The very fact that I was working diligently on my driving avoidance behavior instead of letting it control me kept me encouraged. It took me almost a year of practice before I was ready to tackle 8-e—driving out of town alone—and by that time, I had traveled thousands of miles, one block at a time. Now one of my favorite places to be is behind the wheel of my car, all alone, my thoughts to myself."

There is a definite process involved in changing behaviors. Developing specific skills and practicing your techniques does take time and adherence to the system; but none of this is intrinsically difficult. You have probably been thinking that overcoming agoraphobia *had* to be difficult because of the intensity of the distress you have been feeling. Once again, remember that our habit is to view things as overwhelming, rather than to partialize problems. Be aware that you have the tendency to want to leap ahead, and you will need to practice being patient with yourself as you are practicing your new technique.

There are going to be situations and events on your avoidance list that will not present many opportunities for practice. Rest assured that if you have been successful in achieving comfort levels with daily avoidances, those far-off fears will melt away. For instance, if the thought of plane travel has been giving you trouble in the past but you don't have a trip planned, understand that the skills which have been successful for you on the ground will work just as well in the air. Your new behavior about anxious feelings will have changed your attitude about choice. From now on, you will make choices for yourself on the basis of your needs and your wants, and never again will it be necessary to make a choice for yourself which is based on fear.

*　　　*　　　*

This chapter has given you the nuts and bolts of how to change nonproductive patterns of behavior. The techniques that we have discussed are fundamental and can be used anytime you want to break a bad habit. Agoraphobic behavior is a habit (pattern of behavior) just as smoking is a habit, and you can conquer either or both with what you have learned from this chapter.

Remember:

1) There are four steps for replacing nonproductive habits with productive ones: understanding, planning, believing and doing.
2) It is physically impossible to have an anxiety attack when your mind and body are in a relaxed state.
3) As you begin working on changing what you are

doing, you will also be changing what you are *saying* about what you are doing.

4) There are three important and easy-to-learn techniques to use when confronting fearful situations: ranking, imagery desensitization and in vivo desensitization.

5) Patience and a methodical approach ensure success!

Chapter

13

▼▼▼▼▼▼▼

Making Cognitive or Dialogue Changes

▲▲▲▲▲▲▲▲

MANY OF US struggle with worrisome, self-deprecating, limiting and nonproductive thoughts because we think it is *good* for us to do so. We may think that it is rational, or that it keeps us humble and our egos in check. We may feel that not to do so is to "lie" to ourselves; it may make us quite uncomfortable to give up our negative thinking and replace it with a more cheerful and positive view of the world. What we have to realize is that years of nonproductive thinking have anxiety as a consequence. We do not have to wait passively for our thoughts and feelings to become positive. We ourselves can *intervene* if we have the necessary tools and skills. As you continue reading, you will be introduced to those cognitive and thinking skills which will allow you to take charge and make your days productive.

RECOGNIZING NEGATIVE THOUGHTS

People with severe anxiety make several mistakes in thinking. Some professionals call these cognitive distortions; some call them irrational beliefs. We call them "negative thoughts," and we have put together a list of some of the more common ones for you to consider. Are you in the habit of fueling your own anxiety (and diminishing your self-esteem) through the practice of any of these negative thoughts?

1. I am always nervous.
2. I should know better than this. What is wrong with me?
3. I should be a better parent.
4. What if I pass out behind the wheel of the car and hurt someone?
5. I am different from others and I know they can tell. They are probably talking about me.
6. I should go to church/synagogue (more often).
7. I feel that I don't do a good job because I don't make presentations well.
8. When I tell people about the way I feel, they look at me as if I were crazy. They must be right.
9. If I had enough faith, I would have gotten over this without any outside help.
10. What if I go crazy?
11. What if all the doctors are wrong and there really *is* a brain tumor causing these feelings?

12. I am not much good.
13. What if my children, parents, friends (and so on) hate me? They really have every reason to.
14. I should make more money.
15. All the rest of my life I am going to feel this way.
16. What if my wife gets sick of my condition and leaves me?
17. I should be a better neighbor.
18. I would like to take a vacation, but I am afraid to.
19. It doesn't matter that I've just come from a funeral, I have guests at home and my son graduates from high school tomorrow. I shouldn't feel anxious. I should be able to go through all this serenely.
20. I'm so nervous I can't swallow.

These statements fall into some general classifications: overgeneralizing (1), anticipating (10), concluding (3), exaggerating (20), catastrophizing (11) and ignoring the positive (7). Becoming familiar with these classifications will help you become aware of—and categorize—your own negative thoughts. Go back through the list and categorize the remaining statements. Any one statement may have several of these negative connotations. (We have listed only a few examples—there are *countless* others.) As you are doing this, keep in mind that there is nothing *wrong* with you for having these thought habits. In other words, don't make the mistake of thinking negatively about thinking negatively!

AFFIRMATIONS

An affirmation is a positive statement that you purposefully make to yourself. Sit down with pencil in hand and *think* of five of your most negative assumptions about your life right now. Perhaps you (1) feel helpless, (2) feel dumb, (3) are scared of staying home alone, (4) hate your daily chores and (5) feel unable to change in any way. Before you actually write these down in list form, change them to *positive* statements—affirmations. Your list might read as follows:

1. I am in control of my life.
2. I am intelligent and knowledgeable.
3. I love to be at home and I enjoy my privacy.
4. I feel good when I get my chores done each day.
5. I have the ability to change in whatever ways I choose.

Your next assignment is to imagine feeling what each positive statement says—and to practice that feeling twice a day. Faison typed her affirmations on a card and taped it to the inside of the medicine cabinet. She says: "I didn't want others to see my list because they might have something negative or scornful to say about it; I didn't need any more negatives in my life." In the morning and before bed, when she went into the bathroom to brush her teeth, she opened the cabinet door and repeated each item on the list five times. She tried to relax as she was doing this and made herself feel and believe that each item was true, no matter how far it was from the truth at that moment in her life.

After several days of this routine, morning and night, you will find, as she did, that you have your list of affirmations fairly well memorized. Now you can begin using this technique anytime during the day. Anytime you feel nervous, worried or despondent, you can bring your list to mind and recite it until you begin to feel some difference. The best thing about affirmations is that just doing them gives you a sense of power: you know you are doing something concrete that is good for you. It's like eating spinach—you may not see the result that afternoon, but you know you're getting the nutrition.

If you find yourself forgetting this skill and are having a difficult time with it, immediately add the statement "I love saying my affirmations." Practice until your affirmations have become truth for you. When that happens with any one of your affirmations, substitute a new one for the old one that no longer needs work. For example, if you have been working on the affirmation "I am calm and relaxed while driving" and have reached the point where you *are* calm and relaxed behind the wheel, then it is time for you to replace that statement. Your new affirmation might be "I feel calm and relaxed while skydiving"! (Well, maybe.)

THOUGHT-STOPPING

Thought-stopping is a simple and effective weapon to use against those stubborn thoughts which pop into your conscious mind and stick there. You can stop those weird or frightening thoughts by saying to yourself "Okay, enough!"

or "Stop—now!" Just as soon as you say that, move your thinking on to something pleasant and nonthreatening—a possible vacation, the song that is playing on the radio, the color of the rug, the robin you can see out the window . . . *anything*. The frightening thought will probably return immediately. Repeat your thought-stopping command and consciously change your focus again. It is often helpful to get up and move around, or pick up a crossword puzzle. The trick is to *distract* yourself *while* saying, "Stop."

It is not helpful, productive or realistic to stay worried over disturbing thoughts. It *is* helpful, productive and realistic to say to yourself "Now, this is a frightening thought. All people have them." Use your thought-stopping technique and don't worry about why you had the thought. You know why you had it. You are a human being, and all of us have strange, weird, bizarre, scary, dumb, funny thoughts from time to time. Stop the process of *monitoring* those thoughts. Say "Stop" to yourself silently or aloud, no matter if you have to say it sixty-two times in a single morning. This will eventually become habit, and you will find that it is increasingly easy to dismiss those unwanted intruders from your consciousness.

CHALLENGING IRRATIONAL BELIEFS

This is a favorite tool of Dr. Albert Ellis, and is a technique you can learn to master as well.

Irrational beliefs are those thoughts about ourselves which draw erroneous conclusions. Take Ellis's example of the medical student who failed his boards. The young man became very depressed in the irrational belief "Because I failed my boards, I am a worthless person." That statement represents a leap to an irrational conclusion. "I failed my boards" does not warrant the conclusion that "I am worthless." What was he to do? His choices were (1) to be depressed and feel awful, or (2) to change his underlying assumption. Believe it or not, if you have acute anxiety, you are jumping to one or (probably) more of these irrational conclusions yourself!

In the case of the medical student, you can see that what is making him feel bad is not so much his failure to pass the boards as it is his mistaken assumption about the failure. He may well want to attempt the boards again; he also has the option of reevaluating his career decision. The *issue* is that failing a test does not make anyone worthless. Challenging an irrational belief through mental dialogue is much like a lawyer cross-examining a witness. Discredit that irrational belief until you see clearly that the cause of your misery is your faulty assumption. For example:

IRRATIONAL BELIEF:	"Nobody really cares for me."
CHALLENGE:	So, you think no one cares for you. Yet you have a stable marriage relationship, your children seem concerned and affectionate, your tennis friends call often and your next-door neighbor drops by frequently to chat.

You may need to repeat this exercise over many days before you feel your new rationality taking hold. (This example used practical challenges, but you could also use philosophical ones, such as "People do care for me as much as they can . . . actually, people are mostly involved in their own concerns.")

POSITIVE IMPLOSION

Positive implosion is a technique that we at CHAANGE have adapted specifically for our work with anxiety clients; we know of no one else who uses implosion in this way. In order for this technique to be successful, it must be repeated again and again and then again over a brief period of time. It involves an intensive rerouting of positive time and energy. We use it with people who, for example, have a wedding to attend in just a few days, or who must make a plane trip or drive a long distance, but who may have just begun to learn their new skills and haven't had the luxury of much practice time. To understand how positive implosion can work, imagine that you are the person who has to make the plane trip. Picture yourself sitting in your seat in the airplane. Fix that image in your mind. Picture yourself as calm, relaxed and happy. You feel good about being there; you imagine yourself the way you *want to be*. Do not imagine yourself the way you have been, or the way you are afraid you might be. Try for the very best scenario you can picture. This will not be particularly easy, and you will have to work at it a little. Devote the same amount of time and energy that you would normally spend nonproductively (worrying and frightening yourself) to practicing positive imaging. Positive implosion is best used for *one* specific goal with only a short amount of time to practice. If you find you need to confront a frightening situation *soon* and you haven't been working with your skills long, you will find positive implosion very helpful.

COGNITIVE RESTRUCTURING

Cognitive restructuring is the skill of learning alternative interpretations. In the field of agoraphobia treatment, there are several expressions that are universally recognized as trademarks of the condition: "What if," "I can't," "I'll try" and "but." If you will drop these words from your vocabulary, it is possible that you might get over agoraphobia without doing *anything* else!

We suggest to our anxious clients that they immediately begin to change *every* "What if?" statement to a "So what?" This is more difficult than it may sound; a typical response to that suggestion is "You mean I should say, 'So what if I get in my car, panic and kill an innocent pedestrian?'" As strange as it may seem, it *is* more productive to say "So what if I have a panic attack in the car?" because you will be more relaxed and less likely to catastrophize. Let's look at what you are *really* saying when you change a "What if?" to a "So what?" In the example above, you are actually saying "Well, for years I've kept myself tense, fearing that something could come from these symptoms. Now I know that it is only anxiety. I have been in the car many hundreds of times with no tragic consequences, even though I have often felt that something horrible was about to happen. I am now going to be more positive. I am going to say to myself, 'So what if something unfortunate happens? I'll deal with it then,' but I am no longer willing to limit myself by concentrating on these anxiety-producing thoughts.''

Work on your "What ifs"—do not *allow* them in your thoughts or your conversations with others. When you make a conscious effort to do this, you become aware of the amount of restructuring you have to do, and you can see how you have been increasing your anxiety with these statements. As difficult as it may be at first to change your "What ifs" to "So whats," know that it *will* become easier for you, and that the benefits to yourself and those around you will make it more than worth the effort!

"I can't" is another sly fox. "Can't" connotes incapability and permanent disability. When you use this expression you are setting yourself up for continued limitation. A person with the agoraphobic condition wants and needs to do things that he or she probably *has* done before and is *capable* of doing. No one who is avoiding "doing" something because of anxiety will ever know that he *can* do it again until he *does* it again! Open up possibilities by recognizing that you have not lost any precious capabilities. Instead of saying "I desperately need a haircut, but I can't go to the barbershop," say "I need a haircut, and though I may feel some anxiety, I will not allow that anxiety to prevent me from doing what I need to do. I *can* go." "I can't" is limiting; "I can" is enabling, and is a far better choice of words than "I'll try."

What's wrong with the word "try"? Isn't that a positive word, and shouldn't we all be "trying" every day? The answer is a resounding *"No!"* You've *been* trying—as we all have—and that has not been working too well, has it? There is a marvelous scene in *The Empire Strikes Back* in which Luke Skywalker is trying, without success, to pull the spaceship out of a murky lake. In desperation, he turns to his mentor, Yoda, and asks, "What am I doing wrong? I am trying so hard!" Yoda's answer is, "There is no *try;* there is only *do.*" Doing is the key; trying is not doing. "Try" is tentative and implies that you might not be able to accomplish your goal. Trying is not the point anymore, and it is certainly not a word you want to use in your struggle to get over the condition of agoraphobia.

Agoraphobics use the word "but" so frequently in describing their symptoms that we can almost predict when a "but" is coming. Typically, a person will ask, "Have you ever heard of anybody with dizziness?" "Yes," we say, "that is one of the common symptoms." They reply, *"But* have you ever heard of anybody who is dizzy all the time?" "Yes," we answer, "chronic dizziness can certainly be part of this condition." *"But,"* they go on, "have you ever heard of it being so bad that the room looks tilted?"

These people are trying to let us know how truly horrible their condition is, surely worse than any case we had seen or heard about. They have to show us how severely they had been mistreated and misunderstood: *"But* I *am* different,

and what you are saying could not *possibly* apply to me."
Their saying "but" prevents them from being able to see
any positive alternatives or accept any suggestions.

If you are going to change your behavior, it is essential
that you become *aware* of how much you may be using
"What if," "I can't," "I'll try" and "but." As long as
you're going to be focusing on your dialogue, there are
several additional words that you would do well to discontinue using. Gerald Jampolsky, in his book *Love Is Letting
Go of Fear,* suggests that you eliminate the following from
your vocabulary: impossible, limitation, if only, however,
difficult, ought to, should, doubt. *Decide* that you will
become conscious of your use of these words, and be determined to restructure your thoughts in a way that will not
require them. Like eliminating caffeine from your diet,
eliminating these words from your vocabulary will give you
an *immediate* boost. You will begin to feel freer and less
anxious, and to see how your use of these words has kept
you powerless and tense.

Dr. Norman Vincent Peale may be considered the father
of positive thinking. He is certainly its major spokesperson,
and has created a unique ministry. It has been his mission to
educate people to the fact that they can do better and feel
better *now,* that they can take charge of their mental attitude
now. All his books are filled with suggestions that can be
very helpful to the person who wishes to become more
positive, in thought, word and deed.

Two years ago, Millard and Faison were in New York
City at Christmastime and attended Sunday services at Marble Collegiate Church. Dr. Peale's message was "You Are

Equal to Whatever." At the end of the service, there was absolutely no doubt in Faison's mind that each of us is endowed with the resources to take charge of his or her emotional life and personal happiness. It was a wonderful message and helped Faison reaffirm her own strengths.

We really can take those old, timeworn negative words and expressions and throw them away once and for all. They simply are no good—not for us, not for our children, not for our parents or our friends. They do nothing to help create a healthy, positive atmosphere in which we can grow and flourish. They do not dispel the anxiety. They do not move us forward with energy, excitement and happiness. When you feel that life is passing you by; when you feel that you can never learn to change; when you feel that you are alone; when you feel that others have more fun than you do; when you feel that your family doesn't care—regard these negative thoughts as enemies of your happiness and change them to positive, productive and nonfearful thoughts. You can do it!

* * *

The purpose of this chapter is to help identify those errors in dialogue which are contributing daily to your state of intense anxiety. Here are some points to remember:

1) You can learn to recognize and intervene in negative thoughts and statements that diminish your self-esteem and keep your adrenaline (and anxiety) activated.

2) A very helpful tool is the ability to make affirmations:

consider your five most nonproductive thoughts and then list them, revised to productive ones. If you will practice these statements twice daily, you will soon find that you can call on them at will to help you through anxious situations. The day will quickly come when these statements will accurately describe your life.

3) Thought-stopping is a skill that is particularly helpful for those who are troubled and frightened by worrisome, sometimes terrifying thoughts. Just as a parent would say "Stop" to a child who was about to touch a hot stove, you can learn to say "Stop" to yourself, redirecting your thoughts and consciously focusing your attention elsewhere.

4) Learning to challenge irrational beliefs (assumptions) will help free you from depression. Fight your tendency to jump to negative or catastrophic conclusions by investigating alternatives.

5) Positive implosion is a way of practicing, in your imagination, those feared situations and events that offer infrequent opportunities for practice.

6) Cognitive restructuring is a method for changing those words, phrases and general outlooks that are negative and limiting.

Chapter

14

▼▼▼▼▼▼▼

Learning Assertive Skills

▲▲▲▲▲▲▲▲

To ASSERT is to affirm or profess. To be assertive, you must know your rights and protect those rights when they are threatened. One or more of our rights are threatened daily; this is a part of living. Our views and our needs are bound to conflict with those of others. Philosophically, when we talk about using assertive skills, we mean dealing with those around us from a position of strength, and having the ability to exercise that strength should we choose to do so. To do this, you first need to know your rights as a social human being:

You have the right to state an opinion.
You have the right to say "No."
You have the right to be wrong.
You have the right not to explain your thoughts or
     position.
You have the right to ask questions.

You have the right not to answer questions.

You have the right to say "I don't know."

You have the right to judge your own behavior.

You have the right to change your mind.

You have the right to privacy.

You have the right to accept compliments.

You have the right to change the subject.

Assertive behavior is atypical in agoraphobics; a person suffering from this condition feels that both her strengths and her rights have been weakened. This chapter will help you regain your right to be assertive. Before we explain how, we want to describe more typical behaviors displayed by anxious individuals:

PASSIVE BEHAVIOR

Passivity can be defined as behavior that results in giving up, lying down and letting people walk all over you. If you stifle your thoughts, feelings, wishes and desires, you are being passive. If you hesitate to give your opinion or make your preference known, you are being passive.

An example of passive behavior could be: your mother-in-law calls you on the telephone, late at night. She tells you she is feeling ill and needs someone to drive her across town to the all-night drugstore to fill a prescription. You agree; you get up, dress and drive the few miles to her apartment. She meets you at the door and you can tell she's irritated that you took twenty-five minutes to arrive. You say nothing, not wishing a confrontation. You politely help her into the car and you drive across town, only to find that the drugstore has permanently closed. You know, though, that there is a twenty-four-hour pharmacy at the hospital downtown and offer to drive her there. After all, you're already up and dressed! She refuses, saying, "Just take me home." You oblige.

Agoraphobics often feel powerless and overly dependent on others. These feelings not only generate anxiety and resentment, they result in lowered self-esteem, which causes the anxiety and fear that you wish to conquer. The spiral deepens. You wish to be anxiety-free, so you don't make waves. Because you don't make waves and stand up for your natural rights, people take advantage of you. This creates tension, worry and anxiety. You then wonder what is wrong with you that causes people not to treat you well. You may then try harder, or become angry, or both. This creates stress and anxiety, more body reactions and lowered self-esteem. In the next social encounter, you cower even more, hoping against hope that the person will "treat you right." If he happens to do so, all is O.K. for a little while; if he happens not to, there goes the predictable cycle all over again. Those around you may react to your passivity with emotions ranging from disgust to irritation to superiority.

AGGRESSIVE BEHAVIOR

Many styles of relating to others can be classified under the heading of aggressive behavior. We view the aggressive personality as one characterized by being pushy, quick to talk and act, headstrong and overly self-protective. You snap people's heads off; you yell at your children or spouse; you are rude in traffic; you hang up on telephone salespeople. Aggression is another typical agoraphobic reaction to being powerless, though it certainly doesn't look like it at first blush. Here's how this works for many of us:

You have had a horrible day; nothing has gone right. You weren't able to ride the elevator when you went to see the dentist and you had to take a Valium just to make it through the examination. Your tennis game was rained out; you were delighted because you didn't want to play anyway (you'd said "yes" to a friend only because you couldn't say "no"). Your spouse walks in and says, "How was your day, darling?" You proceed to tell him in no uncertain terms that your day was rotten and, furthermore, so is he! You purposely start a fight with him in an attempt to relieve the tensions of the day. You then go sit down in the family room and turn on television; however, relaxing is now impossible. You feel frustrated. More than that, you feel a nebulous tension and anxiety that is nearly indefinable. But it shouldn't be a surprise when you look at your day. Those around you react with hurt, anger and defensiveness, often feeling both humiliated and revengeful.

PASSIVE-AGGRESSIVE BEHAVIOR

Simply put, passive-aggressive behavior can be understood as any action taken by an overdependent person who is frustrated and unable to deal with the cause of his frustration directly. A secondary consequence to the agoraphobic condition is passive-aggressive behavior because of our over-dependence on those around us for safety and security. An example of passive-aggressive behavior could be:

You have an appointment for lunch with someone who has always made you uncomfortable. You are to meet at a restaurant at twelve noon sharp. You are forty-five minutes late and make profuse apologies for your tardiness. (You didn't have the courage to decline the invitation, so you unconsciously make your friend as uncomfortable as possible.)

What follows is a chart that can be useful to you in identifying your own styles of behavior—passive, aggressive or a combination of the two. As you read this list and each description, make a mental note to yourself of some recent times you have used each behavioral style; ask yourself whether or not you got the results you desired, and recognize that you used this behavior out of habit, not out of rational choice. Most of us, if we really think about it, will recognize that these are not effective or appropriate choices.

NONASSERTIVE BEHAVIORS CHART

MANIFESTATION	DESCRIPTION
One-Upmanship [aggressive]	Always the "authority," those who indulge in this practice correct and revise every statement made by others. Ready to cite examples of their expertise, they seldom listen or learn.

Their favorite conversational gambit is "Can you top this?"

POUTING *[passive]*	"Poor me" behavior, childish in nature and intent. The pouter is waiting to be rescued by the offending party. A low-risk way to say you've been hurt; an attempt to make the offender feel guilty, which rarely works. Usually, it makes the offender feel disgusted.
CONSTANT REMINDING *[passive-aggressive]*	This person tries to control others' lives by reminding them: "Do you feel you *need* another drink?" or "Did you *remember* your mother's birthday?" This is not a straight-on communication, but rather a low-risk, sideways communication.
PROCRASTINATION *[passive]*	A low-risk approach to any activity is to put it off. Most people who procrastinate also worry and stew while procrastinating, thereby using more energy than they would if they had gone ahead and done what needed to be done. Jobs remain undone and guilt and anxiety ensue.
INTENTIONAL INEFFICIENCY *[passive-aggressive]*	In order to irritate authority figures, the individual purposely misunderstands instructions and misinterprets

intentions. The task just barely gets completed, creating tremendous anxiety and inconvenience for someone else.

LATENESS *[passive-aggressive]*	A classic behavior pattern. This person is often late for appointments, frequently late for social events, but shows up with a smile and a dozen roses. What can you say? This really is a "got-cha" behavior and leaves others with unspoken frustration and a sense of your disregard for them.
MARTYRDOM/PAIN *[passive]*	This characterizes people who do for others ceaselessly, volunteering for jobs and feeling worthy and superior at their own incredible charity. They seldom say "no" or ever complain in any straightforward way. Others have to run fast to outdo them and are rarely able to break into their martyrdom—it is a closed system, with the martyr calling the shots. This creates anger and tension, but the martyr loves the pain so much that he hates to give it up.
OBSTINACY *[passive-aggressive]*	This marks the "yes-but" people. They are the first to ask your opinion, standing on one foot, hardly able to

contain their enthusiasm for chiming in the very second you are finished to say why your suggestion is impossible and would never work. They tend to be negative in outlook and refuse to think in positive terms. Life is hard, and they are not going to let you forget it while you are in their presence.

ARGUMENTATIVENESS [aggressive]	Arguing for the sake of arguing, people with this trait will take issue with anything, regardless of their true position. Their only goal is to intimidate others and delight in their discomfort.

If you want people to treat you with more dignity, and if you want to treat *them* with more dignity, take a look at these common anxiety-prone behavior patterns and make some choices about them for yourself.

1, 2, 3s OF ASSERTIVE BEHAVIOR

How do you tell the carpet cleaner that he didn't clean your carpet? How do you tell your guilt-giving mother-in-law that you won't be having guests for Thanksgiving dinner? How do you say "no" to car-pooling for a friend? How do you ask your supervisor for a raise? What do you do when you get a compliment from a friend?

All these situations seem very different from one another, but they can all be approached assertively and with relative ease, if you will remember these three steps:

Step One	Use an empathy statement.
Step Two	State what you want.
Step Three	Suggest an outcome to the other person.

Suppose you have arranged for a carpet-cleaning company to come to your home while you are away. You return home to find that the cleaners have missed the downstairs den (where the worst stains were). What's the issue here? The issue is not that they charge a lot; the issue is not that your neighbor said they were good and that you are disappointed in your neighbor. The issue is not that they promised to come a week earlier, but didn't show up. The issue *is* that they missed a room and that you want them to come back and clean it. Here's what you say:

Step 1	"Mr. Carpet Cleaner, this is ———. You cleaned my house today and I know [empathy] you must be very busy this time of the year,
Step 2	but I found that my downstairs den was missed, and [what you want] I need it to be cleaned.
Step 3	What day this week [suggested outcome] will you be able to complete the job?

It is important to remember that your issue is *only* that you want your carpet cleaned. If you keep your statements direct and nonblaming, it will maximize the possibility that the cleaner will work with you toward that end. Be as flexible as possible about the smaller issues [time of day, and so on] without giving up on the larger issue—getting your carpet cleaned promptly.

Family issues can be touchy. It's November 10 and your spouse's mother wants to come to your house for Thanksgiving. You are at her home when the subject arises. You have had company all fall; there are two birthdays in your family in November, and you don't want to put on a large Thanksgiving this year. What do you say that isn't rejecting?

Step 1 "Mom, you have really been great [empathy] having all of us so often for Thanksgiving over the years,

Step 2 and this year I know that you will understand that John and I have decided [your wants] to have a quiet dinner at home alone.

Step 3 You can certainly count on us [suggested outcome] to plan another family get-together soon.

You don't have to complain about how busy your life is and has been. You don't owe her an explanation of how your life is going. You have shown that you appreciate her past efforts, stated your plans for this year and offered an alternative solution.

Many people, not only agoraphobics, have trouble accepting compliments gracefully, without deprecating themselves. Your best friend calls you and thanks you for coming by to bring her child a birthday gift. She is clearly touched by your gift, and before she hangs up, she blurts out, "Joan, you are the most thoughtful and caring friend that I have ever had." What on earth do you say?

Step 1 "Harriet, thank you so much for saying that; it really makes my day." This is really all you need to say. If you choose to add a further statement, it could go like this:

Step 2 "I have always valued your opinion."

Another example of assertively accepting a compliment is as follows: "Susie, I love your sweater." Assertively you respond:

Step 1 "Thanks so much."
Step 2 "My sister gave it to me and it means a lot to me."

You are adding to your assertive response by disclosing how *you* feel about the compliment. It is not assertive to negate the compliment by saying, "This old thing? I don't even know why I wore it today." This is a put-down of your friend who likes the sweater, and a passive-aggressive act.

Putting these skills into practice is hard, but being assertive can reduce your anxiety level. Years ago, Millard and

Faison were politically active. At least once a week, Faison would answer the telephone and the caller would be a committee person wanting to speak to Millard. She'd say, "I'll have Millard call you." She'd then nag Millard until he made the call, or resent him for not responding promptly, feeling that it was her job to see that the "right" thing occurred. She learned to assertively say "I'll see that he gets the message" rather than passively say "I'll have him call you." If the caller went on to say, as was sometimes the case, "Will you make *sure* he calls me?" Faison would respond, "I'll make sure I leave the message for him." The interesting thing was that before long, she really didn't care whether he returned the calls or not.

For years, Ann felt it was her responsibility to awaken her children early enough in the morning to give them time to get to school. This usually turned into a battle, with Ann feeling resentful and the child in question feeling angry. Often, the child would be slow and miss the bus, and Ann would have to drive the child to school.

With her two youngest kids, Ann made up her mind early on that it would be their job to arise and prepare for school. If they missed the bus, the rule was that they would not be driven to school. They would take an unexcused absence and Ann would not cover for them. This assertiveness on Ann's part resulted in children who were responsible, were on time and didn't feel angry and resentful. These skills are rarely second nature for agoraphobics, but they are important to acquire. It is helpful to remember that no one in the world is here to look after you except you, and if you don't look after yourself, it probably won't get done. If you choose to claim your rights, that is good. If you choose to be passive, you are going to pay the price by feeling put-upon and unappreciated. If you choose to lash out in an aggressive, demanding way, you will pay the price by feeling frustrated.

*   *   *

Remember:

1) Assertiveness is not so much a tool as it is a philosophy. The bedrock of that philosophy is understanding your rights as a human being. Those rights are yours, but it is up to you to guard them; it is not up to others.

2) There are four styles of behavior that are generally recognized in relation to contact with other persons: assertiveness, aggression, passivity and passive-aggressive behavior. The severe anxiety sufferer often uses these last three kinds of behavior to deal with uncomfortable situations. This comes from having felt overdependent as a result of the years of fear and limitation due to agoraphobia.

3) There are many habitual nonassertive behaviors that each of us has used. Too much reliance on any one of them is nonproductive and will keep you from getting what you want out of life.

4) The way to use your assertive skills is to remember the three-step method: first, use an empathy statement; next, state what you want; then, suggest an outcome. Use of this method will give you the best possible chance of producing a win-win encounter for both parties!

Chapter

15

▼▼▼▼▼▼▼

Letting Go

▲▲▲▲▲▲▲

LETTING GO is the therapeutic goal for all agoraphobia/anxiety sufferers. If you are to overcome your severe and incapacitating anxiety, you *must* learn to let go of fear of the condition.

In moving from immaturity to maturity, from childhood to adulthood, we consciously and unconsciously make decisions about which of our beliefs we will leave behind. The agoraphobic typically has a whole sackful of beliefs and attitudes which weighs him down and keeps him from moving toward recovery.

You may be absolutely convinced that your life would be different, better, easier, more fun and more productive *if only:*

your parents had understood you;
your parents had waited longer to have children;
you had been an only child;

184

your husband/wife didn't have a heart condition;

your husband/wife were more understanding;

your parents had recognized your fearfulness and helped you;

you had been able to apply yourself in school;

you had had ministers who had explained religion to you in a way that wasn't frightening and judgmental;

you didn't have to work so hard for approval;

you had felt capable of having and rearing children;

there were a quick cure for agoraphobia.

These ideas and others like them are strangling you because of your reluctance to let go of them. If they are part of your daily repertoire of thoughts, they will depress you and allow you to place the blame for your unhappiness elsewhere: on your parents, siblings, teachers, friends, society, the church. What an unfair world, and what a shame that all these outside forces are keeping you from functioning the way you want to!

Blame, self-pity and inaction are the enemies of "letting go"; once you can pinpoint their influence in your life, you can begin to make choices about them. When you realize that saying "Oh, well, I'll think about doing that tomorrow" may be keeping you from ever moving toward the kind of life you want, you can then *choose* to push yourself toward new behavior that not only will bring you pleasure, but will also increase your self-esteem. Faison's experiences are good examples:

BLAME

"I had laid both the blame and the responsibility for my condition at my parents' feet. I also may have thought that I would be unable to get over agoraphobia without some change or action on their part. One day, after a therapy session in which I had talked long and hard about the lack of understanding my parents had exhibited, I began to realize that I was beating a dead horse. More than that, they were not at fault. My childhood wasn't perfect; but there is no perfect childhood for any of us, my parents and grandparents included. We *all* remember rebuffs, embarrassments, words that hurt, times we felt wronged and unloved. However, if we *choose*, we can also remember feeling incredibly cared for, encouraged, loved and forgiven. I had forgotten that and had chosen to focus only on negative recollections.

"In order to regain control of my life, I had to let go of my tendency to blame and judge others. Know and understand that letting go of the blaming habit does *not* mean transferring the blame from others to yourself! It means letting go of blaming *anyone*. What happened, happened. It may be unfair that it happened, but it is no one's fault. Blame is paralyzing for you and it will keep you from moving forward.

SELF-PITY

"It was difficult for me to give up self-pity; it was one of my favorite pastimes. I used it in order to feel justified in feeling bad. If you practice this habit long enough, you may find, as I did, that you can even come to enjoy your bad fortune. Let me strongly suggest to you that you will feel better (less anxious, less tense, less despondent) if you will stop feeling sorry for yourself. Your demeanor will change; your interactions with others will be more satisfying. You will look and feel like a new person, able to greet each morning calmly, with pleasure. Self-pity is a powerful enemy who masquerades as an understanding friend. Let it go—it is not helping you to be who you want to be.

INACTION

"We all have a tendency toward inertia, but those of us who develop agoraphobia have been thwarted so often that we have developed the habit of saying to ourselves 'What's the use? Nothing I do seems to make any difference.' Let go of that thought—it's history."

You learned as you read the chapter on changing behaviors that often your viewpoint will change as you begin to *do* things differently. The action itself promotes feelings of well-being and of self-satisfaction. It's not always necessary to "think" before you "do." Begin by doing little things that will give you a sense of accomplishment. Write a long-overdue letter to a friend, mow the front yard, organize the top drawer of your desk, fix that skirt you could be wearing if only you would put a new zipper in it, make a list of short-term goals for yourself. It will be impossible for you to doubt your productivity!

We need to let go; we need to forgive; we need to move on. How do we go about it once we have decided to do it? If you are using this book the way we hope you are, you have already done a lot of list-making. It is now time for you to make the most important list of all. This is a list you will make only once. Using as your springboard the list of "unfairnesses" on pages 184–85 (which was actually Faison's), make your own list. Make certain that it is *comprehensive*. Take as much time and use as much paper as you need—you don't want to overlook a single grievance! As you are doing this, notice the way your body reacts. You can *feel* how these thoughts affect you; your body demonstrates it dramatically. Is it surprising that holding on to these feelings is contributing to your anxiety? Once you have completed your list, read and consider each statement and commit yourself to letting go of its power over you. After you have conscientiously studied your list, decide how you will *dispose* of it. The more dramatic the method, the greater the impact. If you have devoted a lot of time, thought and emotional energy to the list-making process, the act of destroying the list will be a meaningful and liberating experience.

If you have worked your way through this book, you are now in a position to unwind the spiral of agoraphobia. Reconsider, if you will, the characteristics of the personality type that is prone to developing agoraphobia. You are sensitive and intelligent by nature; you were reared to be perfectionistic, to push for control, to fear rejection and to worry. It was probably during your early adult years that your stresses became such that your body began to react to them with periods of tension and episodes of panic. At that point, *you* responded to those body reactions with fear, dread and worry, not with calmness and understanding.

We want you now to let go of those earlier reactions. They were of another time and place and are no longer appropriate for you. We want you to embrace a positive outlook and productive dialogue about your life and your expectations for the future. We know that you can let go of your need to control all things, and that you will realize that true control lies in the way you react to things that happen, not in controlling the happenings themselves.

We encourage you to let go of being sad that your life has been less than perfect, and of feeling that you have been shortchanged. Come to the realization that you are a neat person and that a significant part of your character is the result of things not always having been perfect for you!

You no longer have to allow your body to frighten you. You can recognize its signals and respond in a caretaking way whenever you feel anxious, when your body gives you signals indicating that you are under stress and need to slow down. In order to manage your stress, you must spend some time and energy understanding how your body reacts to stress and what you need to do to relax, say "no" and regain control.

If you choose to let go of all that is nonproductive, the peace and calm that have been eluding you will be yours at last, filling in the gaps left by the dissipating tension, worry, anger, dread, anxiety and fear. Letting go means taking charge, accepting responsibility and, most of all, giving up the battle against the fear. You have learned everything necessary to *let go of the condition itself!*

Chapter

16

▼▼▼▼▼▼▼

Putting It All Together

▲▲▲▲▲▲▲▲

WE'RE AWARE that you are probably reading this book straight through before converting it into a program for yourself. With each page you have turned, you have hoped that we were going to insert a few grams of magic and you wouldn't have to do the real work involved. We know that you are sick of hearing us say that the magic is in the doing, but just to prove us right, we have asked three graduates of the CHAANGE program to allow us to show you what they were able to accomplish. We are quoting directly from the evaluations that they filled out, as well as from letters each has written to us.

CASE HISTORY #1: Matthew Harris, single, age twenty-two

From "Pre-Program Evaluation": *Give us a brief descriptive paragraph on how you view your condition.*

November 2—"I want to get rid of this phobia permanently. Since I feel I developed my condition because of my lack of self-confidence, I'm concerned that CHAANGE's program may deal only with my symptoms and not with the cause. I am, however, ready and willing to put all my efforts into the program and see what happens. I fully expect to get over this phobia; I just hope I've chosen the best program to accomplish that.

"In January of 1982, I began seeing a counselor for some dizziness I was experiencing. It wasn't a physical problem, but at the time neither my counselor nor I recognized it as agoraphobia. After two months, I stopped seeing him because I didn't feel he was helping me that much. We did focus in, though, on the source of some anxiety—my relationship with my parents—and that was a positive step. The dizziness subsided temporarily."

From "Mid-Program Evaluation":

January 26—"I know I'm getting better, even though I go two steps forward, one step back. I'm listening to my relaxation tape [part of the CHAANGE program] ten times a day and practicing it in my head too. One problem I'm starting to run into regarding relaxation is a squeezing sensation in the middle of my chest. I'm able to relax my *muscles* through progressive relaxation, but this squeezing sensation isn't the result of a tight muscle. I do find, however, that when my attention begins to focus on something else, the feeling goes away.

"As far as working on avoided situations: I haven't practiced my imagery desensitization as often as I'd like, but I now feel comfortable doing two of my least anxiety-provoking situations. Another hindrance to my progress is lack of opportunities to practice. I don't have a car of my own yet, and getting out to practice *some* of my avoided situations is difficult. For instance, how do I practice my new skills when getting in front of an audience to perform? This is my most anxiety-producing situation, and while I haven't reached that situation in my desensitization process, I know I will need to eventually practice that.

"P.S. I'm considering moving to another city. Would it be detrimental to my progress with CHAANGE to make such a move around, say, the ninth session?"

From "Post-Program Evaluation":

March 25—"I do not consider myself as 'agoraphobic' any longer, even though I haven't accomplished all my goals. It struck me the other day that I will never become agoraphobic again—even if I tried—because I know what it is; I know it's I who have control over the way I react. This was relieving and enlightening to me. I do not avoid going into any situations. I have completely overcome my fear in four or five situations, and am currently working on the others. I realize now it is just a matter of time and practice before I'm totally finished.

"Agoraphobia is no longer scary to me since I know exactly what it is and how to deal with it. Thank you, CHAANGE."

We received the following letter from Matthew on July 2:

"I feel really proud of myself today. Last night I went to

that agoraphobia support-group meeting here in town to talk about CHAANGE's program and how much it helped me. Some of the members had been through other programs; some were taking drugs; but none had ever been through CHAANGE.

"Speaking in front of a group of people has been my most feared situation, and last night's meeting was really the first time I've had the opportunity to practice going through that particular situation. (I don't think I could have picked a more sympathetic group of people to practice in front of!)

"So, actually, two different things were taking place at once for me at that meeting: (1) [it was] a chance to let other people know about CHAANGE, and (2) [I had] an opportunity to practice.

"I planned my day carefully so I would have the best possible chance of succeeding. The week before the meeting I dialogued *constantly* with myself, telling myself that I loved performing in front of other people, and that I was relaxed and self-confident as I did. I also physically relaxed when I thought about it. I took a two-hour nap before I left, since I knew I'd be using up a lot of energy practicing behavior and attitude changes.

"Then a series of unexpected things took place that could really have thrown me if I'd allowed them to. First of all, the car I'd planned to drive to the meeting was suddenly out of commission. Instead of getting myself angry and upset, I tried to find another car to borrow, which I did. Right before I left, I listened to the relaxation tape. I was nervous, but I kept assuring myself it was normal anxiety and perfectly okay. As I accepted it, it tended to go away.

"After I got on the freeway, the gas light went on, letting me know I was about to run out of fuel! I told myself, 'If I run out of gas, I run out of gas. There's at least enough to get me where I'm going, so I'm not going to worry about it right now!'

"As I merged into the interstate highway, what to my wondering eyes should appear but a rush-hour traffic jam! (Which, by the way, is my second-most-feared situation!)

"So there I was, sitting alone in my car in 85-degree weather, stuck in a massive traffic tie-up and on the brink of running out of gas! What did I do? I laughed. The chance of all these 'incidents' happening at that particular time was about a million to one, but they happened anyway.

"I think my being able to see the humor in my situation really eased things up for me. Of course, I talked *diligently* to myself the whole time in a positive way, using a lot of 'So-whats,' etcetera. Looking back on everything, it wasn't at all the 'catastrophe' I would have imagined it to be.

"Well, I made it on time to the meeting anyway. I was nervous as I began talking to them, but it went away after five or ten minutes, and it was *all* normal anxiety.

"As I told them about CHAANGE's program, they seemed surprised at two things in particular: (1) that fearful feelings are caused by fearful thoughts, and (2) the number of times I listened to the relaxation tape as I went through the program.

"I don't mean this in a self-righteous way, but I felt kind of sorry for them. Not because I didn't think they could get over agoraphobia, but because *they* didn't think they would. Most of them took the attitude that it's just something they'd always have to deal with because 'That's just the way we are.' They actually believed that their personalities were fixed in cement, and that changing their nonproductive habits to productive habits was impossible.

"Most of them admitted that they didn't practice much, yet they were confused as to why they still hadn't gotten over their condition. I felt that this support group was much more interested in *talking* about their symptoms, and *talking* about how to get well, than in actually doing something to make it come true.

"I made as many helpful suggestions as I could, recommending certain techniques they could try, but I don't think I reached most of them, and I felt a little angry because of it. I wanted them to know all the things I've learned with you, but at the same time, I didn't want to come across as dogmatic and turn them off. I realize you can try to help a person only so much; then it really is their responsibility to accept it and work with it.

"As I left the meeting, I felt so proud of myself; I can't adequately express it on paper. I saw how far I had chosen to come in comparison with some of the people in the group, and I just felt great about myself! I went through my most-feared situation successfully, and I saw how much my life has changed in only six months because of the way I now look at myself and the way I think about things.

"I'm sure you've heard this a thousand times before from other ex-CHAANGERS, but thank you so much for the opportunity to change my life for the better. I will never be the same as I was before I found CHAANGE; a whole new world has opened up to me, and part of it is because you and Ann cared enough to reach out and help other people. I'm looking forward to doing the same.

"Thanks to you, and everyone you work with. You guys are great!"

CASE HISTORY #2: *Betty Lewis, married, age thirty-eight*

From "Pre-Program Evaluation":

August 5—"I had about four panic attacks two years ago. Last August I moved from North Carolina to Florida. I have gotten more depressed as the year went by. In June, I slept almost not at all for eight days while I was home in Virginia visiting my parents. I felt panicky most of the time. July 5, I went to a psychiatrist, who put me on antidepressant drugs. I have slept since then. July 25, I talked to H.F., got the relaxation tape and have done it ten times a day since then. I am better.

"I had individual and marital counseling for about two months several years ago. D.E. has been suggesting your tape program to me on and off for about two years."

From "Mid-Program Evaluation":

October 11—"I am driving two hours to Tampa once a week, spending the night in a motel alone and coming back the next day. I still have some neck pain driving, but it is not as severe. I have begun to work on a Ph.D. So far, I am handling the stress of school better than I have [at] other times because of the relaxation tapes and the weekly tapes.

I had a bad night of anxiety this week, but that's the first in a long time. If I get through exams and papers calmly, it will definitely be different behavior for me. I feel happier and calmer, more able to enjoy each day, not looking back longingly, or forward with fear.

"I had company and did not get upset.

"I give in to negative thoughts sometimes, but they used to be constant and now they are occasional.

"I am seeing a therapist because my depression got so bad this summer. Without the CHAANGE program, I do not think I would be able to hang with the therapy. My anxiety about the therapy is reduced by the CHAANGE program. You are giving me more 'how-tos' for how to change than he is. He keeps holding me to the fire of needing to change, though. I do not want you to send him a progress report. I think I'm picking up vibes from him that only he can help me. Maybe not—a lot is happening with me emotionally when I'm there, so I may be reading the situation wrong.

"CHAANGE is a great program and I am glad the tapes and material are in my possession. There's a sense of security in knowing I could do it all again if I fall apart again."

From "Post-Program Evaluation":

"I am fine, happy, not panicky or depressed. I drive two hours to school once a week. I am doing much better at controlling myself and not other people.

"I have never been able to take a nap, but if I do three consecutive playings of the muscle-relaxation tape while lying on the floor, I feel rested and renewed. I do that most days.

"I have not been to my psychiatrist since early November. I suddenly started to get better with CHAANGE. He did not celebrate my improvement the way I wanted him to, so I have not been back."

Betty's letter to us dated March 18:

"I finished the fifteen-week program in late November. I knew one of my final tests of my new skills was to fly somewhere. In December, I decided I would go on my husband's company trip to Acapulco in March. Until then I had said I would not go.

"I usually get very agitated packing for a trip. All that day, I lay down on the floor and did my relaxation exercises every time I got shaky. As time ran short, I kept deciding not to do things that did not absolutely have to be done—like washing my hair. It was too oily for comfort, but I could do that after I got to the hotel.

"The most helpful to me of all the suggestions by CHAANGE is to say the five sentences at the end of relaxation. Negative thoughts were my constant companions. Now the new dialogue is in my head always—even in the middle of the night when I go to the bathroom, I say my adapted version of the sentences:

'I enjoy being free of worry, fear and anxiety.'
'I enjoy every day.'
'I like knowing I have a choice about how I live and how I study.'

'I enjoy the challenge of practicing new behavior.'
'I like being in charge of my life.'

"I was calm through the takeoffs and landings to Texas and then Acapulco. Right out my hotel window I saw people parasailing (on a parachute pulled by a motorboat) over and over again. I kept saying to myself 'I enjoy the challenge of practicing new behavior' as I walked to the sand to see the procedure close up. Without feeling fear, I paid my ten dollars, was strapped to the parachute harness and took off. High over the blue waters and rocky coast of Acapulco, I said my sentences, felt the wind and peaceful stillness of being airborne. As I was landing, the men below shouted, 'Let go! Let go!' I spread my arms and legs and truly 'let go' as CHAANGE has taught me to do."

CASE HISTORY #3: *Joanne Fairley, married, age forty-two.*

From "Pre-Program Evaluation":

July 10—"At this point, it [agoraphobia] is not as severe as it once was—say, in my twenties and thirties. At one point, I couldn't even walk the long drive we had to the mailbox. I've been doing basically what is suggested on my complimentary tape [sent when someone requests information about CHAANGE]—doing the things I fear, trying desperately to change my reactions to things. But it is always with me. I am elated when I achieve a marked degree of success [even though] I don't always. I just think I have it licked and 'wham' it zaps me again. This makes me feel so totally defeated, as I'm trying *so hard* to overcome it."

From "Mid-Program Evaluation":

August 30—"I view my condition now as something I can and will get over. I was amazed to learn how angry I was. There was a situation in my home re: one of my sons—anger stored up for over ten years. I was finally able to vent it, get rid of it—calmly and realistically—and talk with him about my feelings.

"I am driving more—going to malls more. Not completely comfortable, but more so than ever before. The avoided situation I'm working on presently is driving. Grocery stores don't bother me at all anymore. I've gone out to eat a lot; just close to home at first, and with someone. Now I'm going farther and farther away and find I am stopping for longer periods of time. I am not getting panicky as frequently. Having a *hard* time with negative feelings, but am working on it daily.

"I have a hard time getting the [relaxation] tape in ten times a day, but will try to improve on this as I realize it is necessary.

"Your letter about doing those things came at a perfect time. I needed the nudge right at that particular time. Have had company for two weeks. It was difficult to get away from everyone to do my exercises and tapes in private. Every time I'd shut my bedroom door, someone would come beating on it."

At this point in time, Joanne has not completed her program, but we wanted to let you enjoy two of her delightful letters to us:

September 3 (Joanne's first letter to CHAANGE):

". . . I just wished to share this with you if I may.

"As you know from the Labor Day weekend, my area was engaged in a very real hurricane threat and emergency situations. I reside in P.C., two miles from the coast, eight miles from Treasure Island, twenty-five miles from Tampa.

"Fortunately, I live sixty-two feet above sea level at my particular location and was not forced to evacuate. However, my seventy-six-year-old father lives on Treasure Island, about twelve miles from me. At 2 A.M. Saturday, I drove this twelve miles in gale winds, alone, through a roadblock to get my father out—I, who am afraid to drive in broad daylight five miles from home alone in the best of weather conditions. I *was* terrified. I kept using my relaxation techniques; they didn't work extremely well, so I began singing. My choice of songs was ridiculous—'Deck the Halls.' It was the only song I could think of at that particular point.

"*This* time, I couldn't call my husband to 'rescue' me or 'take over' for me, as he was called in on emergency duty at midnight, two hours prior to my dash into the elements.

"I had fear, but I 'floated' with it—all the time praying that I and my fear wouldn't float right on out to sea.

"Later, I had a houseful of people. At one point, we were an island, totally cut off and isolated. As you know, that's one of our biggest fears (besides losing control), not being able to get *out* of some place. Well, I got through it—without one panic attack and with *no* Valium.

"I don't know if it is my involvement with CHAANGE

these past couple of months—as if I finally had a *real*, legitimate fear—not just something I could not identify—as if my desire to get my father was so strong it overrode my fear—or if my husband wasn't available—or a combination of all of the above.

"For the *first* time in my life, I realized it *was* O.K. and normal to be afraid and that's all it was. I don't like being afraid, but I realized that everyone else was afraid also, and for once, I was not 'different.' Whatever, I still can't believe I did that. And dealt with being afraid the entire weekend—and dealt with it very well, if I do say so, as I was terribly afraid.

"Today, I drove back to Treasure Island in the sunshine—alone. (My father went home yesterday with friends.) I walked to the seawall behind his house by the bay, sat under an oak tree comfortably—enjoyed the now calm, serene waters, as if the weekend had never happened—but it did, and I was there, alone, thinking of a fallen maple leaf gently drifting in a clear mountain stream. At that particular moment, I felt more relaxed than I can ever remember feeling. . . ."

September 20—Joanne's third letter to CHAANGE:

"Well—I'm sharing things *again*. Every new thing I learn is equivalent to a major discovery—to me. I know the world is just waiting with bated breath to learn what great things I'm up to—Ha Ha. Of course, I realize this isn't exactly so, but I'm going to write you about them anyway. Sort of like keeping a running journal of events.

"I did something I never thought I would do. It's a very

simple thing, but not to me. On several occasions, I've noticed I have actually taken the initiative and taken the responsibility for my own needs. It is so true, the things you discuss in the tapes. I would always wait around for someone else to 'take care of it' or to get me out of whatever predicament I made for myself.

"First off, I decided to have a garage sale. I never would've or even could've considered that. All those strangers—I'd be 'trapped' in the garage—the list goes on and on. Seems real important to me to clear out my clutter—all the cobwebby old things in my mind as well as old useless things I've kept around inside and out. Maybe it's symbolic of the stage I am entering. For whatever reason, I decided I was going to do this—and I'm full well expecting to have fun doing it. And, if I don't, that's O.K. too. (Besides, I need the extra hundred dollars to pay my last installment in the program—Ha Ha.)

"Also, last week I drove to P.S. Mall and stayed a couple of hours. I went off Monday with friends and stayed all day. I make little short trips here and there if I feel like it. If I don't, I don't go. Instead of saying 'Oh, why couldn't I have done that?' I say 'I'll just do that at a more suitable time.'

"My 'What-ifs' are changing to 'Probably won'ts.' (I still haven't convinced myself completely of the 'So whats.') I'm working on it. My Valium intake is on the wane, but I still take 1/2 on occasion—like Linus trying to part with his security blanket. However, I am pleased I've been able to do this much and I'm not beating myself up if I take a couple steps backward. There's lots of tomorrows to come. I know I can't blindly rush through this, racing, hurrying to get through this—and like an Olympic runner carrying an extinguished torch. When I cross the finish line, I want *my* torch to still be burning! The *positive* things and goals I used to have inside me once, I want to still be there.

"Another new phase—I have desperately wanted to have a part-time job for a long time. Of course, all my self-imposed roadblocks prevented this—only the 'wishing' remained active. Well—now I *want* it. I don't think I am ready to go ahead with this totally unencumbered—yet. I envision it a lot. So, I've taken a mini-action on it. I once was a legal secretary and a good typist. Well, I put an ad in the paper to do typing at home. I have a good typewriter—it's a start. It's a productive action. I went and replenished my typing supplies and didn't tell anyone I was doing this till after the fact. I just did it. I already have four regular customers and hope to get more. It is not stressful work to me—I enjoy typing—I always have.

"I had won an art scholarship in high school I never did anything with. Well, I got some art supplies, set me up a makeshift 'studio' in my guest room—just strictly for my own enjoyment and relaxation—and have begun painting and sketching again.

"I've become interested in many old interests again. I've been frequenting dozens of craft shops in the area. I'm countrifying my house. I've met people interested in Early American reproductions and Americana. Sometimes we go searching for finds together.

"I went for an eye exam way down in 'P.' Well—

actually ten miles away; to me, it's 'way' down in 'P'—get reading glasses I know I've needed for five years.

"See—it's little, itsy things—but I haven't been so involved or more interested in things—or actually *enjoyed* thinking about tomorrow, and content with my todays—in *so* many years. And to know I am working *toward* things and not being bogged down *with* things. I feel I am gradually being released from a prison of sorts. I'm letting myself feel things I always blocked off. I'm letting myself screw up and I'm letting myself be *human*.

"I truly do have something to offer. I don't want to allow fear to ever put out my torch again.

"I still have a long way to go, but now I am enjoying the journey. Teaching someone to 'let go' has got to be the greatest gift you could ever give to anyone.

"When I think back to even a few short months ago, the change in my thinking is drastic. My family is noticing it too. I've had more help and assistance. My nineteen-year-old son was actually scrubbing the bathroom and doing his own laundry; my twenty-two-year-old son actually *moved out*—Hallelujah!! (Several months ago, I wouldn't have admitted *deep elation* to that for anything.) My twenty-three-year-old son has visited more in the past two months than he has in six years. I feel good about this one. My husband and I are on new wavelengths—this too is good!

"P.S. I *still* want a part-time job outside the house. My approaching it this way and doing typing at home—for now—in no way diminishes my eventual goal, which I honestly expect and believe at some point [down] the road, I will be able to fulfill."

*　　*　　*

As you read the comments and letters sent to us by Matthew, Betty and Joanne, you must have sensed a gratitude on their part for the process offered by CHAANGE. It is probably only natural for us to react in a thankful way anytime we gain insight or learn from another person. However, it was not the program in which these fine people participated that made the difference in their lives. No therapy, no program, no book can change what is going on inside you. Matthew, Betty and Joanne succeeded because they were tired of anxiety and willing to make some changes in their lives. As you read their letters, we hope you could see how well each of them applied their new behaviors to very different lifestyles. They each fashioned their own specialized coping skills from those we have discussed in this book. Putting skills together, and then putting them to work, is exciting and fun—not to mention *rewarding*.

Chapter

17

▾▾▾▾▾▾▾

So, What Is Recovery?

▲▲▲▲▲▲▲▲

RECOVERY IS BEING ABLE to plan your day without having to worry about whether you will feel too anxious to function. Recovery is no longer caring whether or not you become anxious. Recovery is *not* being totally calm and tension-free for the rest of your life—no one is that way. Recovery is understanding that if you feel anxious, you will know (1) what is happening physically and emotionally, and (2) what to do and what *not* to do.

When you have recovered you are where you always wanted to be: in a position to choose not to spend time and energy worrying about a future anxiety attack that may or may not happen. You may never experience panic again. You have learned to recognize stress and to eliminate superfluous anxiety by: relaxing; using productive dialogue; continuing to be active in the things you may enjoy doing; getting plenty of rest; eating properly (eliminating excess caffeine and other stimulants from your diet) and cutting off any added worry behavior that you are practicing. It seems simple because it *is* simple. Making it more difficult is an *old* personality habit that is not worth reestablishing.

You are probably concerned about the possibility of a setback. You worry that no matter how much you improve, there will always be the chance of a recurrence. You may even refrain from practicing your most-feared situation because it "could" precipitate a dreaded setback. Setback is a negative, fear-laden term which only means that you have had an episode of increased tension for a period of time. If you should experience this, it's no big deal.

We think the statistics we have gathered over the years are indicative of the recovery you can expect. Seventy-five percent of our program participants are married. Eighty percent of our male graduates are employed, as are 52 percent of our female graduates. For females, this figure is 2 percent above the national average—a very interesting statistic for a group of people once thought to be "housebound"! Typical agoraphobia victims are normal, ordinary people who manage their families, work for a living, get married and divorced and live to ripe old ages just like everybody else in the world.

Eighty-one percent of the graduates of our program, in a self-report survey, said they no longer experience the disturbing anxiety symptoms. Let us underscore that statistic by saying that 81 percent of our graduates *no longer* consider themselves to be agoraphobic or limited by anxious feelings. Another 14 percent have moderate anxiety, and only 7 percent rate themselves as significantly bothered by anxiety. Of this 7 percent, only 1 percent say that their anxiety symptoms are "very severely disturbing."

We cite these statistics to illustrate that anxiety has not had the power to rob you of your personhood. That core person—creatively intelligent, competent, dependable, perfectionistic, sensitive and likable—has always been there. Fear simply became so important to you that you forgot to take inventory of your equipment to find that it was all still in place and could not be erased by self-doubt.

Both of us got over agoraphobia, and we have helped thousands of others to do the same. Once you have overcome agoraphobia, not only are you able to manage anxiety, you are *super*-able to manage anxiety. The very fact that you have suffered and recovered from this condition has given you, unlike others who have never known severe anxiety, a unique opportunity for personal growth and exploration.

We recognize that this may sound smug and that you may be saying, "Easy for them to say." We believe that every human being has within himself the power to achieve recovery through personal growth. We ourselves did not gain all our personal growth from the skill mechanisms in this agoraphobia recovery process; however, it was the springboard, allowing us to see that there were all sorts of possibilities open to us. We began to experience our sense of power when we saw that we could participate in our own recovery.

The first step for us was seeing that it was possible to take charge and grow beyond this condition. Once we dropped our armor of protection (our avoidance behaviors) our resistances fell away and our learning process began in earnest, never ceasing to amaze us at how opportunities *come to us*.

You remember the illustration in Chapter 3 of the personality factors, rearing factors and inherited characteristics that fueled the development of agoraphobia. Now let's look at another illustration, this time of the new you—the you following recovery.

You came into this world with these GIFTS:

SENSITIVITY • CREATIVE INTELLIGENCE
OPENNESS

As a child, you probably experienced:

Instability/Alcoholism • Critical Rearing
Emotional Repression
Fear of Mental Illness • Separation Anxiety

The adult you have become is characterized by:

The need to be in CONTROL • Fear of Rejection/Judgment
Perfectionism • Intellectualizing/Worrying • Dependability

Enter:

STRESS OVERLOAD

PANIC

PANIC

PANIC

PANIC

PANIC

AGORAPHOBIA
The <u>Learned</u> Anxiety Reaction

Here you are now:

FEARFUL

LIMITED

You
begin
the
recovery
process by:

Being motivated
to change

Understanding your role
in this process

Enlisting your sense of humor

Recognizing the normality of your
feelings

Accepting the need to please yourself.

You become increasingly:

Dependable
Sensitive/Caring • Capable/Competent
Able to Be Assertive • Excited About Growth

And ultimately become that person you have wanted to be:

COMFORTABLE • MATURE • CONFIDENT
ABLE TO TAKE RISKS • CALM • NONJUDGMENTAL
NO LONGER FEARFUL

AND . . .

. . . **ABLE** to use that inborn

SENSITIVITY • CREATIVE INTELLIGENCE
OPENNESS
as you continue the lifelong process of
PERSONAL GROWTH.

As a further example of recovery, look over the following list of agoraphobic attributes and corresponding recovery attributes.

AGORAPHOBIC ATTRIBUTES:	RECOVERY ATTRIBUTES:
suggestibility	understanding of normality
unrealistic worry	active concern
unrealistic assumptions/catastrophizing	acceptance of life with good and bad
inadequacy/perfectionism struggle	feeling of self-worth
preoccupation with body	knowledge and acceptance of mind and body and how they function
illness	wellness
fear of rejection	confidence
seriousness about everything	sense of humor/easiness
need to please others	need to please self first/desire to help others
childishness	maturity
fear of (resistance to) change	quest for knowledge/excitement about growth
undefined anger	ability to confront appropriately
dependency on others to solve problems	knowledge that the solution is within us
frantic approach to life	calmness

We have told you a lot about ourselves and our agoraphobic experiences. We searched our memories and relived some unpleasant times so that you can trust that we do understand just how devastated you have been by agoraphobia. For a long time, we felt that our growth out of the condition was a gift, and one that was impossible to give another. Our continued learning convinced us that personal growth isn't a gift, but a right. We may not be able to make you claim your right to happiness, but we can certainly show you how to begin. We hope our book has given you the impetus you were searching for.

Neither of us likes endings, so please let us hear from you. We want to delight with you in all your successes.

Write to:

Ann Seagrave
Faison Covington
CHAANGE
2915 Providence Road
Charlotte, NC 28211
phone: (704) 365-0140

▼▼▼▼▼▼▼

Annotated Book List

▲▲▲▲▲▲▲▲

BOOKS FOR YOUR PERSONAL GROWTH JOURNEY

Angelou, Maya. *I Know Why the Caged Bird Sings*. The author writes of her childhood and early adulthood years as the daughter of two rather unusual parents. Her insight and warmth are contagious, and you are sure to admire her after you've read this book.

Benson, Herbert. *The Relaxation Response* and *Beyond the Relaxation Response*. Dr. Benson's first book on relaxation came out in 1975 and has been a benchmark ever since. He added his second book ten years later, exploring new dimensions in personal power. They are definitely recommended reading for those who want to learn more about the interaction of the physical, the emotional and the spiritual.

Burns, David. *Feeling Good*. We strongly recommend this book to anyone who is experiencing feelings of depression. The author takes the cognitive approach to helping you "feel good."

Buscaglia, Leo. *Personhood: The Art of Being Fully Human*. This book takes you through the stages of maturity in humans, providing information and insight into not only the stages themselves, but the meaning that can come to us as we grow in life.

Cousins, Norman. *Anatomy of an Illness*. The author writes of his struggle to participate in his own recovery from a seemingly hopeless illness. His writing has inspired many to hope.

————. *Human Options*. A book for the person who wants to browse through the thoughts and feelings of Cousins— a special treasure.

Dowling, Colette. *The Cinderella Complex*. A good book for women who are interested in exploring the idea of gender dependency.

Ellis, Albert. *A New Guide to Rational Living* and *How to Prevent Your Child from Becoming a Neurotic Adult*. Both these books by Albert Ellis give specific guidelines to help us change nonproductive thinking.

Frankl, Viktor. *Man's Search for Meaning*. A life-changing book. The concept of choice is presented in an entirely different and freeing way.

Gaylin, Willard. *The Rage Within*. An excellent book on anger in modern life. Written in an easy and informative style, this book may change your views and answer many of your questions on anger, resentment and rage and their physical manifestations in the body.

Jampolsky, Gerald. *Love Is Letting Go of Fear* and *Teach Only Love*. These books are short and easy to read, but are long on truth. Dr. Jerry Jampolsky is well known for his work at the Center for Attitudinal Healing in Tiburon, California, with children who are cancer patients. You will surely love these books, as we do.

Kasha, Al. *Reaching the Morning After*. Al Kasha, the Oscar-winning songwriter ["The Morning After"], suffered with agoraphobia. He describes his personal struggle and triumph in this book.

Kiev, Ari. *A Strategy for Daily Living* and *A Strategy for Success*. In these two books, New York City psychiatrist, Dr. Ari Kiev, guides the reader through a planned series of exercises (of thought and action) designed to enhance the experience of living.

Kübler-Ross, Elisabeth. *On Death and Dying*. A classic about the stages of death and dying. This book views death as a stage of life and presents its findings in warm, nonclinical terms.

McDonald, Paula and Dick. *Guilt Free* and *Loving Free*. The McDonalds present a husband and wife's view of guilt and sexuality, using anecdotes and examples. There are suggestions on how to live without the encumbrances that guilt, worry and "shoulds" can carry.

Norwood, Robin. *Women Who Love Too Much*. Absolutely marvelous—should be read by every adult woman reared in an environment of alcoholism or other dysfunctions. The insight gained from reading this book could prevent (or help you correct) a disastrous relationship.

Peale, Norman Vincent. *The Power of Positive Thinking*. A specific guide to the value of taking charge of one's own life and problems and, in so doing, how to "let go" of worrying and blocking one's energies.

Peck, Scott. *The Road Less Traveled*. A psychoanalyst writes an account of his and several of his patients' growth. An exceptional book.

Prather, Hugh. *Notes to Myself* and *A Book of Games*. In *Notes* the author chronicles his journey through the growth process. It is presented in little vignettes and notes written to himself as he learns and grows. His second book is a compilation of games or exercises for adults who wish to examine and challenge some deeply held attitudes.

Rogers, Carl. *On Becoming a Person*. This book describes how we can develop as fully actualized individuals. A warm, insightful book.

Rubin, Theodore Isaac. *Overcoming Indecisiveness*. For persons who have trouble making decisions and who wish to become more skilled in this important area.

Selye, Hans. *The Stress of Life*. This book is the classic cornerstone of much of the work that is now being done in the field of stress-related disorders.

Viscott, David. *How to Live with Another Person; The Language of Feelings* and *Risking*. These books speak to us about the issues of everyday life and how we can productively view them and grow with them.

Woititz, Janet Geringer, Ed.D. *Adult Children of Alcoholics*. This book gives basic, factual information about the personal attributes and behavioral styles of people reared in alcoholic homes. It provides clear models for understanding much about how and why people interact with the world in the way they do. *Adult Children of Alcoholics* is highly recommended.

BOOKS FOR THE CLINICIAN OR THOSE WHO WANT TO READ ABOUT TECHNICAL ISSUES

Among the books listed below you will find the many current trends and themes in anxiety and agoraphobia treatment today. These are listed for reference purposes:

Agoraphobia, Edited by Dianne L. Chambless and Alan J. Goldstein, Wiley and Sons, 1982. A survey of opinions on cause and treatment of agoraphobia, including obsessions, marital issues and in vivo exposure.

Agoraphobia, Nature and Treatment, Andrew W. Mathews, Michael C. Gelder and Derek W. Johnston, The Guilford Press, 1981. This book was edited by clinicians in Britain, where much of the original research and clinical work on agoraphobia was done. It gives a good view of agoraphobia, relapse issues, cognitions and insomnia. Included in this book are various rating scales and testing measurements.

The Anxiety Disease, David V. Sheehan, Charles Scribner's Sons, 1983. Strong biochemical emphasis, but does reflect a multidimensional view of acute anxiety conditions. Has received much press because of its widespread influence regarding drug treatment and the concept of "endogenous anxiety."

Anxiety Disorders and Phobias, Aaron T. Beck and Gary Emery, Basic Books, 1985. One of the best books available on the cognitive view and treatment of anxiety. It includes many specifics and a good theoretical treatment of issues.

Biology of Agoraphobia, James C. Ballenger, Clinical Insights, a monograph of the American Psychiatric Press, 1984. A text on protocols for administration of various medications, plus statistical outcomes of certain research studies.

Hope and Help for Your Nerves; Peace from Nervous Suffering; Agoraphobia: Simple Effective Treatment, Claire Weekes, Bantam Books. All Dr. Weekes's books are in paperback and are popular descriptive accounts of how agoraphobia feels and what steps individuals may take to help themselves.

Your Phobia, Manuel D. Zane and Harry Milt, American Psychiatric Press, 1984. Dr. Zane is the director of the White Plains Hospital Phobia Clinic in New York State. He founded "contextual therapy," a specialized in vivo treatment system, and he expounds it in this book. In addition, he provides general models for understanding and treating phobias.

▼▼▼▼▼▼▼

About the Authors

▲▲▲▲▲▲▲▲

FAISON COVINGTON AND ANN SEAGRAVE, both native North Carolinians, reside in Charlotte, N.C., with their families. Each suffered with, and recovered from, agoraphobia and helped design a successful treatment program for the condition. They have been active in CHAANGE (The Center for Help for Agoraphobia/Anxiety through New Growth Experiences) since its founding in 1979.